The Post Nest Plan

Bobbi Chegwyn

Disclaimer:

The information provided in this book is intended for general educational purposes only and not to be a substitute for professional advice, diagnosis, or treatment. The author and publisher of this book are not liable for any damages or negative consequences resulting from the use of the information presented in this book. The reader is solely responsible for their actions, and the author and publisher are not responsible for any harm, injury, or loss resulting from using the information presented in this book.

The information presented in this book reflects the author's personal experiences and opinions and should not be considered medical advice. The author and publisher do not intend to diagnose, treat, cure, or prevent any disease or illness, and the reader should always seek the advice of a qualified medical professional for any health concerns. By reading this book, the reader agrees to these terms and conditions and assumes all responsibility for their actions and decisions.

Contents

Dedication

I dedicate this book to my father, Ray Chegwyn, a true guiding light in my life. Your unwavering support, wisdom, and strength have inspired me, and I am forever grateful for our time together. Though you are no longer with me, your memory continues to guide me through life's challenges.

You saw the best in every situation, and your spirit was unbreakable. Your teaching of onwards, upwards, and always was a testament to your determination to keep moving forward, no matter what obstacles came your way. Your strength in the face of adversity is a quality I strive to embody each day.

Writing this book and serving other empty nesters has been my lifeline in the first year after your passing. It has helped keep my head above water and my mind away from the figurative 'sharks' that often get too close. Your legacy lives on through me, and I am honored to continue to serve others in your memory.

I will carry on with the strength you embodied until we meet again. Your light will continue to shine through me, and I will always be grateful for the love and guidance you gave me.

I hope this book will be a tribute to your strength, compassion, and spirit. I miss you so much, but I know it's time to let you go now.

This book would not exist without the two that made me a mum: Emily, and Lucy. Becoming your mother was the most incredible privilege and blessing I could ever ask for. Always remember, there is no greater love than a mother for her child.

Forever in my heart,

Bobbi / Mum x

A Note from Bobbi

I am someone who has been where you are. As a fellow empty nester, I understand the mixed emotions of watching your children leave the nest and embark on their journeys. It's a bittersweet moment, and feeling overwhelmed and uncertain about the future is okay. But I'm here to tell you that the next chapter of your life can be as fulfilling as the last.

The Post Nest Plan is a book written for you with the hope that it will help you discover your passions and purpose as you navigate this new phase of life. I share my journey and the lessons I've learned in these pages. I share the tools and strategies that helped me move forward and find fulfillment after my children left home. I wrote this book because I believe you deserve to live a life full of joy, purpose, and passion. And I know it's possible, even when it may feel the opposite.

So, I encourage you to take this journey with me, and let's discover what the next chapter of your life has in store.

Introduction

Hello, and welcome to the first day of the rest of your purposeful life! I can't tell you how glad I am that you have chosen to join me in going from empty nest to personal best. I believe that with intention, action, and dedication, this book will bring positive momentum and give you a bird's eye view of the possibility and excitement that can be yours in this phase of life that we are now facing since our children have left home.

So, I'm curious. How did this journey start for you? Were you as shocked, blindsided, and confused as I was? I think parenting is so constant and busy that I never really had time to think about the challenges coming my way when in-person parenting was done. In fact, the only thing that ever crossed my mind was the thought of space and freedom during times of stress.

How wrong I was.

Empty nesting for me came swiftly without care for preparations, goodbyes, or easing into the idea that both my daughters would now be ten thousand miles away from me in Sydney, Australia. At the same time, I remained in Ohio, where my husband is currently working. I remember it so clearly; it's one of those defining life moments I know will always stick with me. My last remaining child at home was preparing to return to Australia at the end of November 2021. We had a plan and thought we had time to pack, say goodbye to her life in the US and get our heads around her move. However, as the quote goes, *"Life is what happens to us while we are making other plans."* On November 6, I was advised by my family back in Australia that our father's health was failing and that I'd have to return home immediately.

In less than 24 hours, we booked a flight, packed up what we could of her life here, and headed home. It was figuratively like ripping that band-aid right off. Ouch! I spent three weeks in Sydney, settling her in and acclimatizing her to the Australian way of life. I also got to spend a lot of time with my father, who, in fact, did a one-eighty and would return home from palliative care in November and live for another five months, eventually passing away on Easter Sunday, 2022.

I remember returning to the US home I had shared with my youngest and my husband and just losing it – completely. For the first few days, I could not stop crying. It was so painful – everything reminded me of Lucy and our shared experiences. I would admonish myself for not being forever mindful over the last 19 years and cherishing every second, whether good or not so great. I really placed a lot of pressure on myself! I was lost. I just existed for the next seven months or so, treading water to save myself from drowning in the sea of grief that was the loss of my children and the loss of my father. I was resentful, I was angry, I was hurt, I was lonely, and I had no direction. I did my best to 'be normal' in front of others, but it took effort. I honestly thought my life was over, and there was nothing else to live for. I expected my paralytic body and numb mind would just shut down at some point, and I'd move on to an afterlife.

I cannot tell you what date it was, but one day in early June, about six months into this experience, I was lying in bed wondering how on earth I would get up and get through that day. It was always such an effort. No fairy godmother appeared at the end of my bed, no angelic being told me that everything would be great, but at that moment, I chose not to let this situation beat me. I knew I needed to be more than the lesson I was experiencing. So, I started with appreciation and gratitude.

These words are all over social media; I have read about them for years. I always *thought* about appreciation and gratitude, but the problem was I needed to *feel it* and bring it totally into my heart space. Positive change does not come from what we think about; it comes from how we feel about what we think about.

From there, that feeling became a light that shone like a beacon from my heart space and quite quickly illuminated my world. I saw, indeed saw, and more importantly, connected with what was around me for perhaps the first time in my life. I didn't see what we may label 'big things.' There was simply appreciation to be found in nature's detail, people's hearts, and what I already had around me.

Appreciation made me feel good for a moment. So, the next day I decided to do more. I felt the tiniest spark of hope, and that's all that was needed. Over the following days and weeks, this energy of hope grew into moments of gratitude that created changes. From these changes, I saw new possibilities and, in time, came to believe in them. And then I stumbled across three magical words in my journey that have allowed me to move from hurt to find happiness, from anger to find peace, and from pain to smile again. I call it my *Secret Success Statement,* and I'll share it with you soon!

In the research I've been conducting on empty nesting, I've come to see that feeling alone and lacking connection is a struggle for many moms. I'd like to share some information to let you know that you are not alone. It was estimated that 3.6 million students in the United States graduated from high school in 2020 and even more in 2021. The number of high school graduates who immediately enrolled in college is around 66%. That equates to around 2.3 million parents and guardians in the United States alone who may be stoically getting on with the busyness of life while inside, they are experiencing shock and turmoil. Then, apart from those staggering numbers, you also have parents whose children have moved away from home for different types of further education. Perhaps for work opportunities, maybe they wish to travel, or simply because it's time for them to expand their wings and fly.

These statistics are just the tip of a global, emotional iceberg on a topic that no one really prepares you for. You need to hear me right now when I tell you, "You are not alone. You are heard, you matter, you are understood, and you are supported. I hear you."

From chatting with women like me, like you, they had this to share about their experience with being an empty nester:

I lost sight of who I was when the kids were young, which caused me to feel a huge loss when they left the nest.

I should have taken the time to date and make friends when the kids were home because I'm very alone now.

I wish I had known how much it hurts. I could have tried to prepare myself for it, but it was a shock at how much it affected me. I still miss her four years later!

I miss the good old days.

I wish I had not taken it for granted that they were home with me. Now they are out living their lives, and I am here in this quiet house.

If I knew what I know now, I wouldn't have thought doing things with friends or with my husband way more often was selfish, but preparing me to be a better mom now in this stage and not a blubbering needy mess.

My daughter is my world, and now I don't know what to do with myself.

I wish I had hobbies and friends other than just my kids.

Maybe their comments resonate with you. Maybe it might feel like you've found your tribe of like-minded women. I hope so! The Post Nest Plan book and its associated activities will assist you in reconnecting with yourself and rediscovering what you enjoy so that you can build your post nest life plan and rock the reignited you!

Again, a warm welcome to your home of change. It is time to choose to be more than the challenge you're experiencing. Together, we've got this, so let's fly!

The Post Nest Plan book is a comprehensive guide that aims to help you rediscover and reconnect with yourself apart from your role as a mom. The book is based on my signature system, the **3 As for Change.** I created these three components to teach others how to be, do, and have the life they desired in 2013. When I was at my lowest after becoming an empty nester and experiencing such pain, loss of identity, and a general disconnection from life, I took these three steps to bring myself from lost to found again. I'm so glad that I get to take you through them!

The book has activities and exercises that aim to enlighten and encourage optimal self-discovery. These activities are designed to be fun and thought-provoking and are best completed in a dedicated notebook. Writing notes in a specific notebook allows you to keep track of your progress and reflect on your learnings.

Before we begin, I have a small task for you. I'd like you to pledge allegiance to your plan. You might wonder, *why exactly we are doing this?* Well, there is value that comes from making a pledge.

Pledges are often associated with commitments or obligations but can also be a source of inspiration, motivation, and trust. Let's look at some of the benefits of pledging allegiance to your post nest plan.

Pledging can be a great way to motivate yourself. When you make this pledge, you set a goal for yourself and commit yourself to achieving it. This can give you a sense of purpose and direction and motivate you to act toward your goals. By making a pledge, you also hold yourself accountable for your actions, which can help you stay focused and disciplined.

Secondly, making a pledge can be a source of inspiration for others. When you pledge your allegiance to your post nest plan and follow through, you can inspire other empty nesters to do the same. You can motivate others to set and achieve their own goals. This can create a positive ripple effect, where your actions inspire others to act toward their aspirations. Pretty cool, hey?

Next, pledging can help you overcome challenges and obstacles. When you pledge, you acknowledge that there may be difficulties or obstacles in achieving your goals. However, by making a commitment, you are also demonstrating your determination and resilience in the face of adversity. When you keep your pledges, you show yourself and others that you have the strength and perseverance to overcome challenges.

Lastly, making a pledge can bring a sense of fulfillment and satisfaction. When you make a pledge and follow through on it, you experience a sense of accomplishment and pride. This can boost your self-esteem and confidence and motivate you to set and achieve even more ambitious goals.

Pia's Story:

As an empty nest mom, I felt like my life had lost its purpose. For years, my focus was raising my children and providing them with a happy home. But now that they were all grown up and had left home, I felt lost and unsure of what to do with myself. That's when I stumbled upon the Post Nest Plan. It was filled with activities and exercises to help me identify my passions and interests and create a plan for the next phase of my life. At first, I was hesitant to start. I wasn't sure I had the energy to tackle it. But something inside me pushed me to give it a try. It was either that or to remain feeling this way. I made my pledge to read the entire plan and do all the associated activities.

The first few weeks were tough. After being 'Mom' for so long, I struggled to identify what truly made me, me, and I felt frustrated and lost. But I persevered, and with each activity,

I better understood myself and what brings me joy. There were some highs along the way, like when I discovered a love for painting during a workshop, joined a hiking group, and rediscovered the beauty of the outdoors. But there were also tough truths that I discovered about myself, like when I realized I had been neglecting my health and needed to change my lifestyle. Despite the challenges, I kept going. I promised myself to see the plan through to the end, and I wouldn't let anything stop me. And slowly but surely, things started to fall into place. I started volunteering at a local shelter, giving me a sense of purpose and fulfillment. I also started taking yoga classes and eating healthier, which improved my overall well-being. And I even started a small business selling my paintings, which brought me a sense of pride and accomplishment.

Looking back on the journey, I am amazed at how far I've come. I have a clear sense of purpose and direction and feel excited about the next phase of my life. And it's all thanks to the Post Nest Plan and my commitment to seeing it through. If there's one thing I've learned from this experience is that it's never too late to start anew. With a little bit of courage and a lot of determination, we can create a life that brings us joy and fulfillment, no matter what stage of life we're in.

So, are you ready to make your pledge to create your post nest plan? I encourage you to take a sheet of paper and handwrite the following and sign it. There's something about the act of putting pen to paper that can help us process our thoughts and emotions in a way that typing on a keyboard simply can't replicate. Studies have shown that handwriting can improve memory and cognitive function and can even have a calming effect on the brain. To enhance your pledge even more, take a selfie with your pledge and post it on your social media profile with the hashtag *#postnestplan*

Your Pledge:

I, [your name], pledge to call on my inner strength, determination, and personal power to go wholeheartedly into self-inventory and self-discovery to create my purposeful post nest plan so I may succeed to the best of my knowledge and ability as an empty nester. I will ask for help when needed, honor all emotions that come up during this process, and embrace all that is me for all that will be my new life.

[your signature]

Lastly, before we begin, through my research over the last year into empty nesting, I have discovered that it is a connection with like-minded others that is on top or close to the top of our wish list.

I would like to invite you to our private Facebook Group, **The Inspired Empty Nest Moms Group.** Here you can post wins, epiphanies, questions, or challenges as you go through The Post Nest Plan.

My focus is on fostering an environment of positivity, one filled with encouragement and devoid of judgment.

There's no room for anything less than kindness and understanding in our interactions. I strongly uphold our commitment to cultivating a respectful, supportive community where you don't just belong, but have the opportunity to truly flourish.

Please note that you can post anonymously once you have joined the group. I'll see you there!

Part 1: Acceptance

Chapter 1
Purging the Pain

Happiness can only exist in acceptance. George Orwell

Life is not happening *to us*; it is happening *for us*. There are lessons to be learned in every experience, every emotion, and every outcome. When faced with the unpleasantness that can appear with empty nesting, there are generally two options — Avoidance or Acceptance.

Avoidance may serve, but only momentarily. The unpleasantness almost always returns. Acceptance (which can get confused with permanence) creates the foundation for positive and powerful personal change. It signals to your mind, body, and spirit that change is desired, so the healing process may begin.

Imagine jumping in your car and not knowing your trip's where or the why. It would be pointless, wouldn't it? We could go here, we could go there, but isn't it just time-wasting without clear direction? Why are you traveling in the first place? Do you even know why, or did it just feel like a good idea to go anywhere? The problem with a broad word like *anywhere* is that it's not defined or detailed according to your personal identity. How do you know it will meet your needs, wants, values, and desires? It's all a bit ambiguous and could have you going in any old direction for hours, if not days... am I right?

Welcome to Purging the Pain. In your very first chapter, you will gain clarity on where you want to go in this next phase of life as an empty nester and why it's important for you to get there. You will discover how life will be for you personally (what you believe, what you think, how you feel, how you will act, and what outcomes you will get) if you *don't* act. You'll also understand the personal benefits to you and your future of purging your empty nest pain so you may move forward, motivated, on the right road, and sure of all you have to gain by choosing to change.

Let's pause for a moment. Think about a time you've stated, "I'm unhappy."

We know what the general term means when one is unhappy, but what does that mean for you personally? What is the detailed version of why you are unhappy? What are you not receiving because of this? How are you unfulfilled? How does it keep you stuck or stagnant in life? How does that affect your relationships with those close to you, your community, or the world around you? How do you know how to solve your problem or purge your pain when it's so ambiguous and undefined?

Now, consider a time when you've stated, "I'm happy."

We know what the general term means when one is happy, but what does that mean for you personally? What is your detailed version of happy? What are you receiving when you are happy? How are you fulfilled? How does it provide you with forward momentum in your life?

How does that affect your relationships with those close to you, your community, or the world around you? How do you know what it is you must be and do to retain happiness? Define your happiness and your future self. Why? Well, you won't find it until you define it. Otherwise, how do you know you've arrived when you get there?

What I want to mention here, and if it resonates with you encourage you take on board as a belief, is that how humans do life is black and white. It is action equals outcome; it is strategies we're running repeatedly. It's a desire followed by consistency to let go of what is not serving us and replace it with something else.

And that's on all levels, from your beliefs to your thoughts, emotions, and actions. If you choose to step out of your emotions and away from yourself for a moment, you can view who you are in life as someone who is doing the best they can at any given moment with the tools, resources, and information they have. If you step back, it can be very black and white and logical. When we view life from an unemotional place such as this, it's easier to take all the pieces that make up your life's puzzle and arrange them to fit in place and create a beautiful picture.

There are three components in this chapter:

1. Discover your personal why when it comes to your desire for change.

2. Connect with your future self about where you wish to travel on all levels (emotionally, spiritually, mentally, and physically) and what life will look like when you have that.

3. Become a super sleuth and open your eyes wide to receive on all levels the evidence that a positive life change can and will be yours.

Let's look at the three.

1. Discover Your Personal Why

This is a deep and defined dive into your current situation without self-judgment and what you believe your life will be like *if you do not change* the unhelpful aspects of it. When you have a clear and detailed look at your current situation and what is not serving you, you will create enough pain and intolerance around the now, providing the initial and vital force you need to entice you to take the actions requested throughout this book. You will be discovering your personal why by way of Automatic Writing.

Automatic Writing is a useful and powerful technique you can use to channel your unconscious mind so you can connect with your higher self (or soul, whatever you prefer to call your own internal guidance system) which can provide inspiration, creativity, and insight in any area of your life. You can uncover any subconscious beliefs, thoughts, and emotions, and the actions you automatically take that lead to outcomes that are good for you or outcomes that are unhelpful in sustaining the life you wish to live.

Settle yourself in a quiet place where you will be uninterrupted. Use a pen/paper or your keyboard. If using an electronic device, close all other tabs and silence notifications throughout this exercise. Take three deep breaths, close your eyes, and set this intention:

I am grateful to connect with my higher self at this moment so she may provide me with insight, clarity, and free thinking without judgment, so I may write for my highest good, my divine purpose, and the best possible outcome.

Set a timer for ten minutes and write about whatever comes to mind. Read what you've written after the timer goes off to see your true beliefs, thoughts, words, ideas, emotions, or images that have appeared. Grab different colored markers, or one will do if that's all you have handy and highlight the aspects that *don't serve you or prove unhelpful.*

2. Connect with Your Future Self

"I have created the life I have; therefore, I can create the life I want." Graham King

Again, this is a deep and defined dive into your situation without self-judgment and what you believe your life will be *if you create change.*

When you have a clear and detailed look at your future self and all you can be, do, and have, you will create enough vital force needed to entice you to take the actions requested throughout your program. We do this by way of Automatic Writing. This will be the same process as mentioned previously. However, when you are done this time, you will look for beliefs, thoughts, feelings, actions, and outcomes that are *helpful* to you.

3. Become Your Own Super Sleuth!

You will train your mind to look for, then in time, automatically find and see the evidence to support you on your journey of change toward your future self. We do this because thoughts of a positive and repetitive nature eventually turn into beliefs. Our beliefs hold power and direct the outcomes we experience. You will do this by becoming your own super sleuth and directing your mind daily to look for 'evidence': the people, the things you have around you, or the thoughts you personally have that will support your desired outcome. Find three pieces of evidence each day.

Think of a tabletop. What is it without legs? Well, it's not a table, is it? It needs something to support it to make it a table, and that is by way of legs. The table legs support the top and make it a table. Similarly, think of the evidence you will gather daily as the legs supporting your table, your future self-version.

Now, I'm not one to perpetually live in a bubble of love, light, and positivity – it's just not human, and it's just not me. However, what I do know is this:

Imagine you walk into a pitch-black warehouse. You have a flashlight with you. You turn the flashlight on and point it toward the back left-hand corner of the warehouse and see a big pile of negativity. You then point the flashlight to the back right-hand corner of the warehouse and see a big pile of positivity.

You then turn off the flashlight and turn on the main light in the warehouse. What do you see? You see that negative and positive will always exist around you, but where you choose to shine your light will impact your beliefs, thoughts, emotions, actions, and, eventually, your outcomes in life. Isn't it more logical to aim to consistently, as much as you can, direct your focus towards good?

Monica's Story:

I have struggled with negative thinking for as long as I can remember. I would dwell on the things that went wrong in my life and constantly worry about what could go wrong in the future. It was a constant cycle of anxiety and stress. But then, one day, I was challenged to look at my life differently. Instead of focusing on the negative, I was encouraged to find evidence of the positives that were already in my life. At first, it was hard. My mind was so used to automatically thinking of the worst-case scenario that it took a conscious effort to look for the good. But as I started actively seeking evidence of the positive things in my life, something began to shift.

I started to notice all the little things I had been taking for granted – the warm sun on my face, the sound of birds chirping outside my window, and the smile of a stranger on the street. I know it sounds like I'm a character in a Disney movie, but I realized there were so many good things in my life that I had been overlooking simply because I was too focused on the negative. Something incredible happened as I continued this journey. My outlook began to change, and with it, my outcomes. I started to feel more confident in myself and my abilities and began pursuing things I had always been too afraid to try.

I landed a new job that I absolutely loved, started dating again, found an amazing partner, and even started a new hobby that brought me so much joy. And the best part was all of these positive outcomes came as a result of my changed perspective. Looking back, I am so grateful I made the conscious decision to focus on finding evidence of the positives in my life. It has completely changed my outlook and helped me achieve things I never thought possible.

Your Next Steps:

1. Complete the Automatic Writing activity to create enough pain around your now, providing the initial propulsion needed to move from your now to your desired future self.

2. Complete the Automatic Writing activity connecting with your future self, where you wish to travel on all levels (emotionally, spiritually, mentally, and physically), and what life will look like when you have that. This will, in turn, create excitement and possibility and provide you with the further propulsion you need.

3. Each day be your super sleuth and open your eyes wide to receive on all levels the evidence that a positive life change can and will be yours. Find one piece of evidence each day and write it in your notebook. It doesn't need more than a few words; the key is consistently focusing on what you have now that supports your future self.

Next, answer the following questions:

1. What specific current beliefs, thoughts, actions, or patterns that may keep you stuck in the 'now' were you able to identify?

2. How did you find the Automatic Writing activity

connecting with your future self and where you wish to travel?

3. What will life look like when you have that?

4. What does your future self believe and think, and how does she feel and act?

5. From here on in, list the daily evidence that a positive life change can and will be yours.

Chapter 2
The Not-Negative Emotion

Every emotion has its purpose, value, and place in our lives.

I was recently driving myself to the airport to go and meet my husband, who was on a work trip in Chicago. I'd never been there before, so I looked forward to finally seeing this much-hyped city. On the 45-minute journey, I had time to drift off into thought. It started when I was just about to pull onto the interstate. I noticed an emotion in my chest, a feeling of being alone. This had been cropping up for a couple of weeks, and I like to pay attention to them when they do, so I can do a bit of self-analyzing to see what is happening and why it is happening.

It wasn't unusual that this was coming up that morning. My husband had left for his trip two days prior, and the day before, I had already dropped my three dogs off to the carers, so the night before I left, I was alone in the house packing. It was so quiet – no furry little friends were judging me for being a horrible 'pawrent,' preparing to abandon them (they know what's going on when I pull out the suitcase), there was no one snoring in the bed next to me (husband or dogs), it was just silent.

And when I was on the interstate thinking about this and feeling this, I decided not to judge my emotion. It was going to be an *is*, and what I mean by that is, it was in my mind going to be neither good nor bad. Just an is. Maybe an *'emotionism'*? I know that's not a word, but how about we make it one to recognize from here on in that an emotion does not have to control us, and we can direct it by befriending it, learning from it, and treating it like an 'is.' Anyway, while driving, I thought about how we treat ourselves when experiencing what might be labeled a 'negative' emotion.

I don't know about you, but as a human, I will often label them as 'bad,' 'silly,' or 'there's something wrong.' But when I've got my self-help hat on, I believe any emotion is an opportunity for a bit of self-inventory if I'm willing to get over myself for a while. With an awareness that an emotion is showing up, we can then accept that it will be part of us for a while, not forever, but for a finite period. Once accepted, we are then hopefully past feeling the need to push it deep down to ignore it. We can sit with it unjudged. I don't even like to think of what it does to our physical bodies and what may manifest when we push an emotion deep down inside – but I think it's important to learn more about our empty nest emotions so we may *create pain around choosing to not work through our emotions* and understanding the benefits in doing so.

As empty nest moms, we grieve. We grieve for the loss of the following – loss in the way we previously experienced each with our children and within our family life. We are grieving:

Love and Connection

Certainty

Significance

Variety

Personal Growth

Contribution.

Grief is not something to be taken lightly. As we mentally try to process the emotions of empty nest grief, our bodies are in overdrive, attempting to do the same. Some physical symptoms of grief include fatigue, insomnia, changes in appetite, and a weakened immune system. Emotionally, grief can result in sadness, anger, guilt, and anxiety. The body deals with grief by going through a process of mourning. This process is different for everyone and can take a different amount of time. Generally, it involves accepting the reality of the loss, experiencing the pain and associated emotions, and eventually adjusting to a new normal without the person or thing that was lost.

It is important to release our grief because holding onto it can lead to negative consequences. When we suppress our emotions, they can manifest in physical symptoms like headaches, muscle tension, and digestive issues. We may also experience increased anxiety, depression, or difficulty forming new relationships. I have experienced several physical changes concerning grief over the years. Hair loss was a big one, brain fog, for sure. And fatigue, energy loss, and insomnia? Yes! All recognizable.

It's important to befriend your current or occasional grief emotions, turn them into *'emotionisms'* and reap the benefits! You might be wondering, *how do I do this?* This is once again where choosing acceptance over avoidance comes into play.

As mentioned in the last chapter, avoidance may serve momentarily. The unpleasantness almost always returns. There will always be a monkey on your back. Wait, what? If you haven't heard of that expression, let me explain it to you, as I find it's a good visual to keep in mind if we choose not to process our unwanted emotions.

To have a monkey on your back is a metaphor that means to have a terrible burden that you cannot get rid of, to grapple with a problem that will not go away. Avoidance keeps that hairy little guy on your back. When you choose acceptance, you sit with your emotion and say 'thank you.' You choose to accept the physical feeling that comes with the emotion, and you say 'thank you.' You choose to accept the thoughts that come from this emotion, and you say 'thank you.' Perhaps you're thinking about your loss, which meant you once had... 'thank you.' You choose to accept your emotions... again, 'thank you.' Perhaps you are releasing tears, which allows us to release stress and emotional pain. You choose to accept your actions or lack thereof... 'thank you.' Perhaps you need some much-needed rest and solitude.

Why on earth are we giving thanks? There are several benefits to doing so. Every expression of thanks raises our energetic vibration in alignment with receiving good. We will be discussing this further in our next chapter.

Jedd Medefind at cafo.org adds: *An immense array of studies now affirm that virtually every part of a person – our intellect, emotions, physical body, spiritual life, and relationships – is made healthier by gratitude.*

When we choose to give thanks, we experience fewer emotions that can be destructive, like envy, resentment, and frustration. We experience increased alertness, enthusiasm, determination, attentiveness, energy, greater happiness, emotional well-being, and greater physical health — objectively and in how we feel. We experience stronger connections with others, more willingness to help, a happier spousal partnership, more willingness to forgive the wrongs of others and less desire for revenge. Then there's reduced anxiety, depression, stress, stress hormones, lower blood pressure, bad cholesterol, and markers of inflammation. We gain improved sleep quality and duration, increased resilience, and a greater capacity to overcome trauma.

Thank you is an acknowledgment of acceptance. You're not pushing anything away for it only to return as that annoying monkey on your back. And when we're not pushing something down or away from us, we allow it to travel its necessary energetic route: to us, through us, and then naturally – not forcibly – away from us. And what I find personally is that when I've accepted the emotion, I still feel it, but the feeling almost becomes a friend. It becomes something I come to understand, learn from, appreciate, and then farewell. I'm no longer afraid of the feeling. We can 'help the emotion along' by getting to know it as best we can. There's a reason for its presence; otherwise, it would not have appeared. You can get to know your emotion by asking yourself the following questions:

- What does loss mean for me right now? (How do you personally define it?)

- Have there been other times in my life when I have felt something similar?

- What does this emotion want to tell me, to show me?

- Is feeling this way a pattern for me or a go-to strategy?

- What could I change about this process?

- Is there something else that's bothering me, along with the grief I'm experiencing from the loss of in-person parenting?

- Do I feel this way because I don't feel I deserve to feel a better-serving emotion?

- Does anything frustrate me about feeling this way?

- How may it serve me to remain in this space?

- What would happen if I let go of this?

- How do I feel about embracing a bright future?

These answers will be personal to you, and there is no right or wrong. Allow all and any thoughts to come to mind. And after you've sat with emotion for some time without judgment and just thought about it and let it feel its feelings, perhaps you've gained some insight into which current personal belief it's linked to.

Back to that day I was in my personal *'emotionism.'* What if my feeling of loneliness would be my 'is' for today? Could I accept that and honor myself that this is my best for today? No judgment of self, just some awareness, then acceptance, and at some stage, I'll get to the action part – but in the meantime, I won't beat myself up about *'Miss Is'* that presents herself today. She is a part of me that is mourning the loss of the direct, in your face, in the same country kind of love and connection that I had with my children. And that's okay because if she's mourning the loss, it means she once had it, which is truly something to be grateful for.

Once we understand what we're choosing to believe and how that produces thoughts that fuel emotions, we can decide (when we are ready and have had enough of some delicious self-indulgence) what action to take to say farewell to it with gratitude for the learning. It is then time to let go of that which will not serve you indefinitely and gift yourself happiness as defined by you.

Perhaps happiness is newfound strength. Perhaps it's acting toward a fulfilled life. Perhaps it's making new connections with others. Perhaps it's making peace with your past. There is value in giving to yourself, which will consciously or otherwise benefit your children, too. How? Well, may I ask you a question?

Would you lay down your life for your children? You strive to give them unconditional and unlimited love. If children, however old, learn from the words and actions of their parents, isn't it better that they learn from a parent who will not let life's challenges beat them, and from one who chooses to be more than the lesson they're currently experiencing?

If you think that this chapter of sitting with and understanding your emotions might be somewhat challenging right now, perhaps reframe your 'why' and tell yourself you will do it for your children. Allow them to emulate your chosen strength, self-love, motivation, perseverance, and desire to experience a well-lived life. *'Would you die for your children?'* I assume your answer is *'Yes, of course!'* If you would die for your children, would you then live your best possible life for your children?

Sometimes, to bring the new into your life, you must create a space by releasing the current that no longer serves you.

You may need to release hurt to find happiness, resentment to move forward, and anger to find peace, or pain to smile again.

It is said that *'life does not give you the people or experiences you want, life gives you the people or experiences you need: to hurt you, to help you, to leave you and to love you and to ultimately assist you to be the person you are here to be.'* If your current life challenges are an opportunity for your personal growth and your soul's evolution, what could you let go of today to move forward more successfully in your life?

Your Next Steps:

The next time a lower vibrating emotion comes up throughout your day, put aside fifteen minutes to sit with it and see if you can answer the following questions. Remember, there are no wrong answers. Answer only what is true for you!

1. What does this emotion mean for me right now? (How do you personally define it?)

2. Do I feel this way because I don't feel I deserve to feel a better serving emotion?

3. Does anything frustrate me about feeling this way?

4. How may it currently serve me on some level to remain in this space?

5. What would happen if I let go of this?

6. How do I honestly feel about embracing a bright future?

And lastly, from here on in, change your strategy around any unwanted moment by

- Stopping.

- Acknowledging your current emotion.

- Gaining any clarity concerning its current purpose.

- Allowing it to do what it needs to do.

- Giving thanks.

Chapter 3
Universal Energy and Personal Power

The most common way people give up their power is by thinking they don't have any. Alice Walker

You may not have a wand, a hat, or a rabbit, but you have a heart, a mind, and a soul! Learn the Law of Attraction fundamentals and how to benefit from the magic of universal energy to create the life you want. There are three key steps to follow when creating the life you desire. Your thoughts, plus your emotions, plus your actions, ignite the Law of Attraction. The Law of Attraction states that like attracts like.

The Universe always mirrors the thoughts you think, the emotions you feel, and the action you take. Who you choose to be affects your vibration. Vibration is energy, and everything comprises energy, including you. This energy flows positively or negatively. Therefore, it is in your best interest to flow positively, and you will attract more positivity into your life. Let's have a look at those three steps.

1. Focus your thoughts on how you wish your life to be.

To make this step even more powerful, bring your desire into the now by including the words 'I am' into your thought process, for example, *'I am healthy!'* Using *'I want'* is less powerful as it presupposes you do not already have it and keeps your desire out of reach. Allow your imagination to place you at the center of your desire. This is your daydream; allow your mind to run freely and without limits!

2. Your positive thoughts and imagery align your emotions with joy, anticipation, and possibility. Your energy will vibrate positively and at a higher frequency to attract what you want into your life.

3. The Universe mirrors your action or lack thereof. Therefore, it is in your best interests to act toward what you wish to create and have the Universe do the same. Many small steps eventually take you a long way. On the flip side, a lack of action will produce a lack of results.

Let's look more closely into this. Think about daydreaming. When you're daydreaming, you get caught up in all the senses of the experience you wish to have. The sights, the sounds, the smells, the way it feels. You get to choose how the story in your mind evolves, coloring your canvas in any bright color you want. You can amplify sounds, heighten tastes, and intensify smells. It's yours to do as you please.

There are no boundaries on daydreams, and you can let all your senses soar to any height you can imagine.

Often, you will feel all tingly with anticipation. This is precisely the level of vibration required to draw your desires towards you. You cannot hide your energetic vibrations from the Universe. It doesn't matter what you want, how hard you work towards it, or if you put a smile on your face. The Universe will respond to how you are vibrating energetically. Whether you are conscious of those vibrations or not, universal energy will match them. It's therefore important to dream and feel good about your life and desires as often as possible. It is also important to look at what may be preventing you from succeeding, and you may have gotten a glimpse of this in your Automatic Writing in the previous chapter.

Your emotional state may not change instantly just because you want it to change. Certain behaviors and thoughts have been used for years and have become habits. However, we can break habits. We can change. At the beginning of any period of change, you will need to practice becoming the change, becoming the person you wish to be. Although Universal Energy knows if your smile is forced, the key is that you are endeavoring to change your emotional state. With practice, what at first may seem awkward or foreign to you will soon become your new normal, your new way of being. Energy will respond accordingly, so keep going, and don't give up. Trust the power of empowerment.

With consistent, repetitive changes, you can transition into the person you want to be and live the life you want to have. During the first period of changing your vibration to a higher level, you may feel like you're just acting 'as if' you've got something or you've achieved something. That is not only fine but absolutely encouraged. Your unconscious mind may have long-held beliefs about your life, yourself, and your environment. Once you've cleared any negative beliefs from your unconscious mind, a space is created, a vacuum, and it's a space that needs to be filled. So, you fill it with a new belief and way of being.

Like any muscle, you need to build that muscle up. Your mind may be a little unfamiliar with this new belief and way of being, so it needs proof that it now has its rightful home in your unconscious mind. This is where acting *'as if'* comes into play. By acting 'as if' you have something or you are something. Then, the unconscious mind supports your new belief and changes focus. When you focus on something, it appears in the world around you. So, act 'as if,' then be it. Act 'as if', then universal energy will respond 'as if,' too!

This state of 'as if' is like a marathon runner. You may know someone who has set the intention to run a long-distance race or attempted a marathon, even if they've never done it before. They do not start out as a marathon runner, but they act as if they are by getting out there each day and running! Little by little, day after day, they run. Their subconscious mind sees that they are being a marathon runner, so their unconscious mind believes they are a marathon runner. Their unconscious mind is supporting and working in conjunction with the new belief that is being embedded daily.

After repetitive enforcement of acting 'as if,' that person has become a marathon runner. That practice of acting 'as if' in the self-help world is called the Be/Do/Have model. You be the person you wish to be, you do the necessary action to bring it into play, and then you will have what you desire. Be. Do. Have. This is the fundamental basis for the Law of Attraction.

Let's look at being. Think of the person you wish to become. How would they think? Focus your thoughts on your desire. Now, the doing. There is no Law of Attraction without action. Action is part of attraction. Follow your thoughts and focus with necessary action to show the Universe you are committed and believe you are the person you aim to be. Become aligned with the idea of who you want to be with the necessary action it takes to be that person. And lastly, the having: The Universe has seen you focus on who you want to be, and you have followed this up by taking necessary action – therefore, the Universe will reciprocate your thoughts, emotions, and actions by presenting you with your needs.

Some people practice the Be/Do/Have model incorrectly. They think having something will enable them to do something, ultimately allowing them to be someone. For example, having a medallion from a marathon does not make you a marathon runner. What is first required is to BE the runner and then to DO the race that will allow you to HAVE the medallion on completion. The HAVE is just the reward; the BE and DO show who you really are.

Start by 'being' today, follow that with 'doing' via taking action, and then you will 'have'. Many people are limited by their own imagination, and ultimately your imagination is limited by your beliefs about life, yourself, and your environment. Spend a minute thinking of where you may be limiting yourself and limiting your imagination. When your imagination limits you, you allow your ego to take over.

Author Dr. Wayne Dyer states that ego (E.G.O.) stands for *"Edging God Out."* When you allow ego to come into play, you are not coming from a place of connectedness to your God Source, your Universal Energy. You may have thoughts such as "I can't do this" or "I can't achieve that." In those moments, you are stuck in ego, in the human form, and not remembering who you are at your core.

As an extension of universal energy, you are playing your role in the production that is your life for a limited season. A lifetime on Earth is just a blink of an eye in the light of all eternity. You are limitless at your core, in this place, in this space. Your abilities have no boundaries, no conditions. In this space, you harness your ultimate power, connect to your universal source of energy, and manifest what you desire.

Ultimately, when you start imagining what you could achieve, who you could be, and what you could bring about, you need to think like the Universe – BIG! Using your imagination without limitations takes your daydreaming to a whole new level. It crashes through the boundaries of your ego; allows you to go wildly and freely to places you may never have thought possible. Remember, once upon a time, such devices as the Internet, mobile phones, and computers were not in people's scope of thinking. It took someone's imagination to crash through the barriers of their own beliefs based on what was 'reality' and to explore the possibility of their imagination. You need to do this too. Write it down, say it aloud, and remind yourself every moment: you are limitless because you are part of universal energy. The only thing that prevents you from wild imagination is the earthly human ego which states something is too impossible.

Dr. Wayne Dyer said that when we are attached to our ego, we are Edging God Out. When we Edge God Out, our life will be limited. Connect to your God or universal energy source, your core/soul and let your imagination fly freely, limitlessly and go beyond what you have ever imagined.

Angelica's Story:

I struggled with self-doubt and a lack of confidence for a long time. I often compared myself to others and felt like I wasn't good enough. However, one day I stumbled upon the concept of using I AM together with an affirmation, and my life was forever changed.

At first, I was skeptical about the power of affirmations. But as I read more about it, I realized that the power of "I am" was genuinely transformative. I started practicing affirmations daily, repeating them to myself in the morning and throughout the day.

It was challenging at the start for me to come up with affirmations that felt authentic to me. But I started small, saying things like "I am capable," "I am strong," and "I am worthy." Over time, I started to notice a shift in my mindset. I began to believe in myself more and started to take on new challenges.

One day, I was asked to give a presentation at work. Normally I would have been filled with anxiety and self-doubt, but this time was different. As I was getting ready that morning, I repeated to myself, "I am confident", "I am capable", and "I am powerful". I was calm and collected when I got to the presentation. I delivered the presentation flawlessly, impressing my colleagues and even myself.

From that day forward, I fully embraced the power of "I am". I started using affirmations in all areas of my life, including my relationships, health, and finances. I found that the more I focused on positive affirmations, the more abundance, and positivity I attracted into my life.

Eventually, my friends and family started to notice a change in me. They saw how much more confident and self-assured I had become and wanted to know my secret. I happily shared my practice of positive affirmations with them, and they, too, started to see the power of "I am."

Ultimately, I realized that embracing the power of "I am" was one of the best things I ever did for myself. By using positive affirmations to shift my mindset and beliefs, I transformed my life and became the confident, capable, and powerful woman I always knew I could be.

Your Next Steps:

We are now going to go through a Neuro Linguistic Programming Anchoring Technique to Access a Higher State of Vibration. This short meditation is available at **inspiredemptynest.com** under the **Resources** tab.

Ok, let's now begin. I'd like you to close your eyes, take a deep breath and relax. As you relax, I ask you to wander to a place that makes you feel alive, energized, and full of love. It can be anywhere where you feel the most alive and the happiest. It can be a place from your past or a place that you visit now. It may be a place that just resides purely in your imagination. Spend some time in this space.

While you are in this space, I want you to notice what's happening with your body. You may feel light, you may feel tingly, or you may feel your heart swell. It doesn't matter if you feel any of these, all of them, or something completely different – just notice how your body responds when you are happy. This happy, exhilarated state means you are vibrating at a higher frequency. Your energy is lighter, more positive, and more abundant to draw what you want to you.

How did you do with the Neuro Linguistic Programming Anchoring Technique to Access a Higher State of Vibration? What did you notice happening within your body?

Can I let you know a little secret, an even more advanced anchoring technique? Next time you do this short meditation, when you are in a heightened state of bliss and joy, take one hand and use your index finger and thumb to press the thumb and nail area. Why? This will 'anchor' your high vibrating state to the action of pressing your thumb. The same feelings of bliss should arise when you press your thumb again after the meditation!

Chapter 4
The Magic of Appreciation and Gratitude

Gratitude is a magic wand that transforms the ordinary into the extraordinary, the mundane into the magnificent, and the overlooked into the overjoyed.

One part of my change from pain to fulfillment was rediscovering the magic of appreciation and gratitude. I no longer solely focused on outcomes and success; I focused more on directing my emotions – to good. The outcomes and success then come of their own accord. Magic appears, changes happen, and I mostly reside in a new place... contentment.

Now I can imagine for some at this stage, you're thinking, *'It's been so bad, so hard, such a struggle.'* I empathize with you; I really do. That was me from January until early June 2022. My dad was dying in Australia, and I was so far away in Ohio. Three weeks before Easter Sunday, I was by his bedside in the hospital. I felt like I was in a hole I couldn't get out of; it was so awful. But here's what I did for personal change when June came, and I was at rock bottom and in a hole of grief.

If this how, what, where, when, and why chance for positive change resonates with you, I encourage you to try it.

I started with appreciation and gratitude. The concept of appreciation and gratitude always lingered in my thoughts, yet the challenge lay in truly experiencing and wholeheartedly embracing it. In doing so, it took on a transformative quality, manifesting as a gentle light that radiated from the depths of my heart, enveloping and brightening my entire world.

I forged a profound connection with my surroundings, quite possibly for the first time in my existence. It wasn't the grandiose aspects that captured my attention, but rather the intricate details of nature and the treasures already present in my immediate surroundings. In them, I discovered a pure appreciation that resonated deeply within me.

Appreciation made me feel good for a moment. So, the next day I decided to do more. A little more each day until months down the track, I often find myself lost in thought about what I have or can witness. Yesterday it was grass blowing in the wind on the side of the road. The day before, it was connecting with the fortune of having a well-stocked food wrap drawer in my kitchen (weird, huh?).

Appreciation is now consuming me more than any lower vibrating energies. I do go low from time to time, and I allow myself this, I'm only human. But I'm more aware of the *Didn't Work* emotions now, and I know I'm better off directing myself to something different. When I'm in the lower vibrating emotions, I have the opportunity to ask: *"Self, whatcha doin'?"* and aim to gain awareness of the state, which then gives me the opportunity for action – to move myself out, onwards, and upwards.

The power of giving thanks is often underestimated in our modern world. Expressing appreciation and gratitude can make a difference to the recipient and the person expressing it. Expressions of appreciation and gratitude can help us cope with major life transitions such as empty nesting, relocating, and separation, providing validation and strength during times of change.

It can help build empathy in relationships, foster goodwill between people, strengthen communities, and bring increased happiness into our lives. Giving thanks has tremendous potential to transform our lives for the better.

The power of appreciation is a remarkable force that should not be underestimated. It has the potential to create an emotional connection between people, strengthen relationships, and lead to more positive outcomes. Appreciation is important for building healthy relationships and developing trust in others.

It can make us feel seen, heard, and valued, increasing our sense of self-worth. It also helps us to recognize the value of those around us and encourages appreciation in return.

Sonia's Story:

I always considered myself grateful, but one day I had an epiphany: Was I really appreciating all the good things in my life? I had a roof over my head, a steady job, good health, and loving relationships, but I realized I was taking them for granted. I decided to conduct an experiment on myself to see if focusing more on what was around me would change how I experienced life.

I started small by focusing on the beauty of nature. Every morning on my way to work, I consciously noticed the way the sun illuminated the trees or glistened on the lake. I started feeling more present and centered; even my coworkers noticed my newfound serenity.

Next, I decided to focus on the people in my life. Instead of just going through the motions of my daily routine, I started taking the time to appreciate the little things my loved ones did for me. I thanked my partner for doing the dishes, complimented a colleague on a job well done, and expressed my gratitude to my friends for always being there for me. These small acts of appreciation greatly impacted my relationships, and I felt closer to the people in my life than ever before.

As I continued my experiment, I noticed the good things I had previously overlooked. I felt grateful for my cozy bed, favorite book, and morning cup of coffee. I even found myself appreciating the challenges in my life, as they allowed me to learn and grow.

By the end of my experiment, I felt like a new person. Focusing on the good things in my life made me more resilient, positive, and connected to the world around me. I had discovered the magic of gratitude, and I knew that it was something I would continue to practice for the rest of my life.

Appreciation can also improve our productivity and creativity by allowing us to shift our focus away from ourselves and onto those around us. By taking the time to thank someone or express appreciation for their work, we can motivate them to keep going, creating a positive feedback loop that leads to better performance overall.

Expressing appreciation can be especially helpful during life transitions, such as when we feel disconnected from our children. Appreciation helps us remember that even though things have changed, there are still people who care about us and appreciate what we do for them. This appreciation can provide validation during uncertain times, help build resilience, and provide a sense of belonging even when it feels like everything else has changed.

Appreciation can bring joy into our lives and those of others by reminding us how much we have to be grateful for. Taking a few moments each day to express appreciation for the people in your life or something you've achieved will give you a greater sense of purpose and contentment throughout your day-to-day life. Appreciation is truly one of the most powerful forces available at our disposal; use it wisely!

Giving thanks and expressing appreciation raises our vibrational frequency. Energy vibration works by harnessing the power of appreciation to create a ripple effect of positive energy. The act of expressing appreciation and gratitude can shift our focus away from ourselves and onto those around us. This shift in focus allows for an emotional connection to form between people, allowing appreciation to be felt, appreciated, and reciprocated. When appreciation is expressed, the person receiving it can feel seen, heard, and valued, which can increase their sense of self-worth.

This appreciation can also positively impact productivity and creativity as it helps motivate others to keep working hard to receive more appreciation in return. Expressing appreciation can also bring joy into our lives as we take a few moments each day to thank someone or express appreciation for their work, leading to a greater sense of purpose and contentment throughout day-to-day life.

Raising your energy vibration can benefit us in numerous other ways. It can promote better physical health, increase optimism and resilience over time, and improve communication skills through a better understanding of nonverbal cues like facial expressions or body language. It can reduce stress levels through increased feelings of safety and security when we are surrounded by people who appreciate us for who we are. In addition, practicing appreciation can lead us closer to finding deeper meaning in life while connecting us more deeply with nature's cycles – all things that contribute towards living a healthier and happier life filled with love and gratitude!

Practicing gratitude is an important part of maintaining good mental and physical health. There are numerous ways to do this, from setting aside time each day to express appreciation for things in our lives or taking a few minutes each morning to write down five things we're grateful for to simple acts like saying thank you to the cashier at the store or sending someone an appreciation note.

One of the best ways to practice appreciation daily is by keeping a gratitude journal. Each night before bed, take out your journal and write down three things that happened during the day that you were grateful for. This can be anything from a kind gesture someone did for you to being able to enjoy a beautiful sunset, anything that brought you joy or appreciation is fair game!

It's also important to list what happened and why it made us feel appreciated or thankful. Doing this will help you understand your values and the personal 'what and why' behind them. We will be diving more into your personal values in Part 2. Another way of practicing appreciation is through random acts of kindness. A great example would be buying coffee for the person behind you in line or writing a quick note of appreciation for someone who has helped you recently. Practicing random acts of kindness gets us out of our comfort zone and allows us to show appreciation in unexpected ways, which can be highly rewarding for us and those around us.

We can also express appreciation through mindful activities such as taking nature walks, spending time with family and friends, engaging in hobbies that we love, watching comedies, or doing something creative like painting or drawing – all of which can help bring greater appreciation into our lives while reducing stress levels.

One great way to practice appreciation is by taking a few moments each day to be still and recognize all that we have been blessed with. Whether it's focusing on something tangible like our home, job, or relationships or something more metaphysical such as health, happiness, or freedom – take a few moments each day just to be still and appreciate these gifts for what they are – precious gifts worth cherishing throughout life's journey!

Practicing appreciation is a great way to become more aware of the things happening around us rather than being overly focused on ourselves. When we take the time to appreciate our environment, our relationships, and those in our lives, we can start to see the beauty and benefit of each moment. Appreciation helps us to notice our own gifts and others, allowing us to find greater satisfaction in life. It helps to lessen the stress associated with competitive thinking, comparison, and anxiety as it replaces these negative thought patterns with an appreciation for what is truly important – our connections and shared experiences.

Focusing too much on ourselves can lead to dissatisfaction with life if we don't recognize that we are only one part of something larger. This can contribute to feelings of loneliness or even depression when we focus too intensely on 'me' and not enough on 'us'. By practicing appreciation instead, we can open up the space for connection with others which leads to a broadening of perspective and appreciation for all that is out there beyond ourselves.

Moreover, appreciation helps us stay connected with our purpose in life by keeping us mindful of what matters most: creating meaningful relationships and engaging in activities that bring joy and fulfillment into our lives. By practicing appreciation, we create opportunities for personal growth as we start recognizing what truly brings out our best selves – whether it's spending more time engaging in hobbies that bring joy or connecting with like-minded people who help foster personal transformation.

Studies suggest that gratitude has powerful physical health benefits such as improved immune function, increased cardiovascular health, and better sleep quality due to its ability to reduce stress hormones while increasing positive emotions like joy and contentment. Furthermore, gratitude helps us bond closer by strengthening social networks due to its power to increase empathy within relationships – something especially important when facing an empty nest or other major transition points in life!

Overall, taking time each day or week just to be still and appreciate all that you have been blessed with can have profound effects in bringing greater peace into your life, both physically and emotionally. It is indeed a powerful practice for creating balance and increasing happiness levels over time while helping you recognize your true worth!

And lastly, here are some things to consider how truly blessed we are as you take your next steps:

- Many women worldwide have to walk four to five miles per day to get something as simple as water for their families.

- At least 80% of humanity lives on less than $10 daily.

- In North Korea, owning a Bible can get you executed or deported to a labor camp.

- In Cuba, a street sweeper makes an average of $19 per month, while a brain surgeon brings in $22 per month.

- Roughly 27% of all children in developing countries are estimated to be underweight or stunted.

- Forced child marriages are commonplace in some countries.

- Based on enrollment data, about 72,000,000 children of primary school age in the developing world were not in school in 2005. Fifty-seven percent of them were girls, and these are regarded as optimistic numbers. Nearly a billion people entered the 21st century unable to read a book or sign their name.

- In Mauritania, over 4% of the 3.8 million population are slaves.

These facts are not intended to make you sad or guilty but to further reinforce just how much we have to be grateful for. Gratitude, like a lot of other things, is a choice. Will you join me in choosing gratitude daily?

Your Next Steps:

I'd like you to pick what resonates with you from the following to help you practice appreciation and gratitude daily.

Make a Giving Thanks Jar. Dedicate a jar (decorate one, if you wish) and have little pieces of paper ready to write beside it. You may want to make a routine of adding cards to the jar or add items as you wish, each with something you are grateful for. Sit down and read the cards at a specified time or when you need to lift your energetic vibration.

Read books about gratitude. Here are some that come highly recommended!

- *Words of Gratitude for Mind, Body, and Soul* by Robert Emmons and Joanna Hill

- *The Psychology of Gratitude* by Robert Emmons and Michael McCullough

- *Thanks! How the New Science of Gratitude Can Make You Happier* by Robert Emmons

- *A Simple Act of Gratitude: How Learning to Say Thank You Changed My Life* by John Kralik

- *The Gratitude Diaries: How a Year Looking on the Bright Side Can Transform Your Life* by Janice Kaplan

Start a Gratitude Journal. Simply get a notebook and add things you are grateful for.

Chapter 5
The Delight in Decluttering

Decluttering is like magic, it transforms chaos into clarity, creates space for new beginnings and frees us to live the life we truly desire.

In the first chapter of Part 1, we looked at what no longer serves us emotionally. We learned that to create the space for new and good to rush in, we have to let go of the old that no longer serves us. I personally love decluttering my physical space as I believe it signals to universal energy two things:

1. I desire free-flowing energy in my physical space.

2. I am conspiring with my energetic source. I'm acting *as if* and clearing the unwanted, detrimental aspects of my life.

The gift in this practice is that once you create the energetic space (and that is also done with material objects), it allows for God, Universal Energy, Source, or whatever you wish to call it, to *rush right on in.*

Let's start firstly with an overview of the practice of feng shui. Feng shui is an ancient Chinese philosophical concept based on the idea of "conscious occupation" and the harmonization of space, intending to bring positive energy and influence to the people who occupy space in the world. It is a practice that focuses on how energy and objects interact in the home. It is believed that when your home has good feng shui, it encourages positive energy to flow freely and helps create balance and harmony.

Good feng shui can bring many benefits, such as improved mental health, increased productivity, better relationships, and even financial prosperity. The practice of feng shui involves decluttering your space to make it more organized and open. This decluttering process can reduce stress and anxiety by allowing for a clearer mind. When fewer items are in the home, concentrating on what is important is easier without feeling overwhelmed or cluttered. Removing unnecessary items also opens up new possibilities for creativity and relaxation, which can lead to a more productive life.

In addition to decluttering your home for better feng shui, it is important to pay attention to furniture placement. You should try to arrange furniture in ways that encourage positive energy to circulate throughout the house while creating spaciousness at the same time. One example is by keeping pathways clear and open. Avoid placing large pieces of furniture in the middle of the room or blocking entryways. Instead, arrange your furniture along the walls or in a way that allows for easy movement and a feeling of openness. This not only encourages the flow of positive energy but also creates a visually appealing and welcoming environment. Avoiding chaos within each room will help ensure your home feels calm and inviting rather than overwhelming or chaotic.

Positive feng shui also involves bringing nature indoors through plants and other natural elements like water features or artwork with natural themes. These elements will bring fresh air into the home and help promote feelings of serenity and peace within each room. Plants are also thought to absorb negative energy while providing physical benefits such as air purification by releasing oxygen into the atmosphere.

Creating an optimal environment inside your home can profoundly affect how you interact with others outside of it as well. When your home has good feng shui, this positive energy will extend beyond its walls and help manifest success in relationships with family members and colleagues alike! By decluttering, arranging furniture correctly, and introducing natural elements into every room, you'll be able to experience a greater sense of well-being both inside and outside of your home!

Decluttering your empty nest when children move out of the house can be quite liberating and a great way to start fresh. Not only does it improve the look and feel of the home, but decluttering can also bring a sense of peace and harmony that comes with having a more organized space. With feng shui, decluttering helps to create a balanced environment that promotes positive energy flow. By eliminating items that no longer serve us, we open ourselves up to receiving new opportunities and experiences. When we let go of physical clutter, we make room for more meaningful things in our lives, such as relationships, activities, and passions.

The mental benefits of decluttering are just as important as the physical ones. Many people report feeling calmer and more relaxed after clearing their homes. This is because decluttering has been known to reduce stress by helping us focus on what truly matters in life instead of being distracted by material possessions. It can also help us stay organized, leading to increased productivity and better time management skills over time. When it comes to decluttering and its effect on cortisone levels, research has shown a strong correlation between the two. Cortisone is a hormone released by the body in response to stress, and studies have found that those who engage in regular decluttering may see a decrease in their cortisone levels over time.

One study conducted by The University of California investigated how long-term clutter could affect an individual's stress levels. Results of the study showed that participants with cluttered living spaces had almost double the amount of cortisol present in their bodies than those who lived in tidier environments. It was concluded that clutter could increase the production of cortisol, which can lead to higher stress and anxiety levels. This ultimately translates into decreased well-being for those who live amongst clutter regularly. Other studies have indicated that engaging in activities such as decluttering and organizing can help reduce overall stress levels while also decreasing cortisol production. As more attention is paid to physical space, mental clarity increases, leading to less stress and anxiety-induced hormones being released throughout the body.

Decluttering helps create an environment where you can be more organized and productive overall, allowing you to think more clearly without any distractions or disorganization hindering your focus or productivity level. In addition to reducing cortisol levels, decluttering can help improve sleep quality and overall mental health. Studies have found that when physical space becomes messy or cluttered, it can cause you to become overwhelmed with excess stimuli from your environment, resulting in poor sleep quality or possibly even insomnia. When items are neatly organized and stored away properly, however, people tend to feel much calmer and relaxed. Hence, they're able to rest easier at night without having any distractions affect their sleeping patterns negatively.

All things considered, it's clear there's a strong link between decluttering and cortisone levels, with evidence pointing towards regular decluttering resulting in lowered stress levels and improved mental health outcomes overall. By creating a clean, organized living space free of unnecessary objects or clutter, you can manage anxiety better while also enjoying more restful sleep, which all contributes positively towards improving both physical health and emotional well-being alike.

Aside from improving our mental health and the aesthetics of our empty nest homes, decluttering is also an environmental choice. By getting rid of unwanted items responsibly, such as donating or selling them instead of putting them in landfills, you're doing something positive for the planet while at the same time reducing your own clutter! And since empty nests usually mean fewer people living under one roof, there's less electricity needed to power lights and appliances, so you'll save money too!

So, if you're looking for ways to make your empty nest home feel like new again without buying anything new, consider starting with decluttering. You may find that it makes all the difference aesthetically and emotionally! Decluttering your home can be both a daunting and energizing task. Taking on such a big project may feel overwhelming, but decluttering is incredibly rewarding when done correctly.

The first step to decluttering your home is to inventory what's there. To get started, grab a pen and paper or pull out your favorite notebook and make four lists: items you need to keep, items you want to donate, items you can throw away, and items that need repair or replacement. As you go through each room in the house, group similar items together so it'll be easier for you to process later on.

Next, declutter one room at a time instead of taking on the entire house in one shot. This will help prevent you from feeling overwhelmed and allow you to focus on smaller tasks. Start with the most cluttered space in the home first — often, the bedroom or living room — and work your way through the other rooms until everything is decluttered and organized.

When decluttering each room, asking yourself if that item brings value into your life before deciding if it should stay or go is important. If not, then get rid of it! You can donate gently used clothing and furniture or recycle electronics where possible. For items in decent condition but no longer needed, such as books, toys, or appliances, try selling them online (Facebook Marketplace) or holding a yard sale with friends.

As well, don't forget about storage solutions! Investing in organizational tools like baskets, boxes, and shelves will help keep clutter at bay. Organize your belongings using labeled containers so that everything has its own place in your home – this helps eliminate piles of stuff accumulating over time by having an established place for everything when not in use.

Decluttering takes time and effort, but it doesn't have to take over your life! With patience and dedication, anyone can experience the positive effects of decluttered spaces within their homes – decreased stress levels from chaos being kept at bay and giving yourself more opportunities for relaxation and fun activities instead of cleaning and organizing. So don't be afraid – start decluttering today!

Stephanie's Story:

As I watched my youngest child pack up her things and leave for college, I couldn't help but feel a mix of emotions. On the one hand, I was so proud of her for embarking on this new chapter in her life. On the other hand, I couldn't help but feel a sense of loss and sadness as I realized that my role as a mother had changed forever. I was now an empty nest mom.

At first, I struggled with this new phase of life. My home felt too quiet and empty, and I missed the sounds of my children's laughter and chatter. But as the days went by, I realized that this new phase of life also brought with it a sense of freedom and opportunity. I could now focus on my own interests and passions without the constant demands of motherhood.

One thing that I had always wanted to do was declutter my home. With three children and a busy life, it seemed like I could never keep up with the clutter and mess. But now that my children were grown and gone, I had the time and space to tackle this project.

I started small, clearing out a few drawers and closets here and there. But as I began to see the progress I was making, I became more and more motivated. I tackled each room of my home, sorting through my possessions and deciding what to keep, donate, or discard.

It was difficult to let go of some of my belongings. I had held onto so many things over the years, convinced they held some sentimental value or would be useful someday. But as I continued to declutter, I began to feel a sense of liberation. It was as if I was shedding a layer of my past and making room for a new chapter in my life.

As I sorted through my belongings, I also reflected on the memories and experiences each item represented. Some items held deep sentimental value, reminding me of special moments with my children or milestones in my life. Others, however, were simply clutter – things that had accumulated over time without any real purpose or meaning.

Ultimately, I was left with a home that felt lighter and more open. I had created space for myself and new experiences, and I felt more in control of my life than I had in years. The process of decluttering not only helped me to let go of physical possessions but also gave me a sense of mental and emotional clarity.

As I sit in my newly decluttered home, I am grateful for this new phase of my life.

While I will always miss my children and the chaos they brought into my life, I am excited to see where this new chapter will take me. And as I look around at my home, I am reminded that sometimes the best way to move forward is to let go of what no longer serves us and create space for what is yet to come.

Your Next Steps:

Decide on one space that you can focus on decluttering. I would suggest, before embarking on this activity, setting a SMART Goal. We want this exercise to be doable. If it's overwhelming, there is less chance for success. With a SMART Goal, you will ask yourself these questions before choosing which space to declutter for your best possible outcome.

Specific: Have I decided on a specific cupboard, space, or room I will declutter?

Measurable: How long will this take me? Do I have the time to complete this job in the next week?

Achievable: Am I able to attain the outcome I want to achieve?

Realistic: Do I have the energy and resources right now to focus on this particular area?

Timely: What day will I start? What day will I complete the project?

Part 2: Awareness

Chapter 6
The Emotional Guidance Scale

Embrace all emotions, for they are messengers from the deepest parts of ourselves, teaching us valuable lessons about who we are and what we need to thrive.

In Part 2, we will be looking at the skill of taking self-inventory. Self-inventory is the ability to assess the condition and success levels of how our personal human behavior affects different areas of our life.

By looking within and understanding what makes us, well, *us*, and acknowledging our 'go-to' patterns and strategies, we can then adjust beliefs, thoughts, feelings, and actions to align us with the life we want.

With awareness comes knowledge, with knowledge comes wisdom, and with wisdom comes personal power.

Choosing to take self-inventory is a practice for those committed to fully moving into the driver's seat of their life. Your life, and how you experience it, begins and ends with you.

Your ability to obtain an expanded awareness of yourself will create better relationships, a happier life experience, and more abundance in all areas.

Introducing your Emotional Guidance Scale, which we will also call your 'EGS.' Created by Abraham Hicks, the EGS is a tool for helping people to identify and understand their feelings.

The scale includes twenty different emotional states ranging from Joy / Appreciation / Empowered / Freedom / Love at the highest level to Fear / Grief / Despair / Powerlessness at the lowest level. Your EGS has one very simple yet essential role: to guide you to that which is authentically you at the core, and you at your core is your personal definition of joy! That's what we're here for.

The School of Life has many lessons, and I truly believe all lessons are presented so we may find our way back to our joy state.

Let's look now at the Emotional Guidance Scale and all the emotions on that scale.

At the top, Joy/Appreciation/Empowered/Freedom/Love represents the state of being that comes when we align with our higher self and our life purpose.

At this level, we feel capable, enthusiastic, and secure in creating our desired reality.

Joy/Appreciation/Empowered/Freedom/Love
Passion
Enthusiasm/Eagerness/Happiness
Positive Expectation/Belief/Optimism
Hopefulness
Contentment
Boredom
Pessimism
Frustration/Irritation/Impatience
Overwhelmed
Disappointment
Doubt
Worry
Blame
Discouragement
Anger/Revenge
Hatred/Rage
Jealousy
Insecurity/Guilt/Unworthiness
Fear/Grief/Despair/Powerlessness

Abraham-Hicks Emotional Guidance Scale

The Emotional Guidance Scale

However, at the bottom, you have low vibrating emotions such as Fear/Grief/Despair. This represents emotions often felt when faced with difficult situations that cannot be avoided no matter how much energy is expended trying otherwise; leaving you feeling powerless despite your best efforts. It's important during these times to not succumb completely to despair but to try drawing strength from sources within instead.

One way to do this is to ask yourself, *"What would my higher self (my soul) do in this very moment? What would her perspective be on this situation? What emotion would she choose to feel instead? What action might she suggest I take?"* This allows you to step away from the human ego, thinking, and emotion and gain a different perspective. Being the observer of your own life allows for detachment, logic, and planning, then ultimately taking action, resulting in a better outcome.

Detaching and playing the observer role truly allows you to sit in a place of complete stillness. In this place, you are separated from the ego and emotion. You can float in the stillness of peace, clarity, and understanding. When I detach and become the observer in my life, I often get a picture in my mind of being a beautiful, shining white orb floating in space!

What is ego? There are certainly several definitions of this word in the dictionary. However, for the purpose of this book, 'ego' refers to being in the physical form and losing awareness of your connection to your God Source. Remember in Part 1, I quoted Wayne Dyer's definition as an acronym for Edging God Out? The ego is born through our birth into human form.

As a soul, we live with love and all that encompasses – trust, compassion, peace, service, spirituality, and connection. When we are born, we are thrust into a foreign world of confusion, need, and dependability. Our focus goes from within and our power to our outer surroundings, and relying on others to meet our needs. We are dependent on others for survival. We lose complete trust and faith in our surroundings and require the outside world to provide for us. If our needs are not met, fear and anxiety develop. Life becomes less about connection to our God Source and more about the survival of the fittest – in all areas – health, wealth, success, independence, stature, intelligence, and more.

Ego bases thoughts, emotions, and actions on fear rather than love. Thoughts, emotions, and actions based on love do not come from the ego; they come from your soul, your higher self. The ability to be the observer moves you away from your ego and brings you closer to your soul. It moves you away from fear and into love.

Think of a cyclone as living in ego, living among emotional highs and lows that may toss you around like an open umbrella. Now think of the center, the eye of the storm – calm, peaceful, mostly still, going within, being at the center, at the core. This eye is similar to a place where we can sit as an observer and view life from a soul perspective. Being the observer takes you away from your beliefs and reactions towards people and life. It opens you up to the possibility that the meaning you have placed on situations or people in the past may not be the only meaning applicable.

Being the observer moves you away from being an *already always* person. Already always? What does that mean? Well, sometimes we are so entrenched in our own beliefs, thoughts, emotions, actions, and strategies that no matter what the reality may be, we will *always* view something with the same reaction that we have always viewed it. We will *already* be in a place of judgment even before we understand the situation in its entirety. As an observer, you can observe not only your own life but also the lives of others and situations you encounter. You can see from a detached point of view, not an *already always* point of view. Pulling away from the ego, the storm, allows you to watch, listen and learn. It puts you into the train of thinking: *'There is no meaning except the meaning I place on this.'* Therefore, what could this situation mean if you are detached and just watching?

What is happening when you are looking at the person, the emotion, or the situation unfolding? Is it as serious or upsetting as you perhaps thought? Can you gain clarity and insight by being in the position of the observer? Can you take yourself out of the picture and observe from another perspective? Could you possibly observe from a soul perspective rather than amid the human ego?

To understand being the observer, I use the analogy that you, in human form, are part of an intricate production that will allow your soul to learn, grow and evolve while journeying on Earth. Your soul knows its Divine Plan. It has the script; you are learning and delivering the lines!

Elizabeth's Story:

I remember when Bobbi first introduced me to the Emotional Guidance Scale. She told me how it could help me understand my emotions better and shift my focus toward more helpful thoughts. I was initially skeptical, but as she explained the concept to me, I began to see the potential benefits.

I decided to try it and started paying more attention to my emotions throughout the day. I quickly realized that I was spending a lot of time on the lower end of the scale, feeling frustrated, worried, and overwhelmed. This wasn't surprising to me, as I had been going through a difficult time at work and in my personal life since becoming an empty nester.

But instead of dwelling on those negative emotions, I decided to use the Emotional Guidance Scale to shift my focus towards more positive emotions. Whenever I noticed that I was feeling down, I would take a deep breath and consciously try to move up the scale by thinking about things that made me happy or grateful.

At first, it felt a bit forced, but as I practiced it more, it became easier and more natural. I started noticing a real difference in how I felt and approached situations. I was less reactive and more proactive and felt more in control of my emotions.

One day, I had a particularly challenging meeting at work that would normally have left me feeling anxious and stressed. By using the Emotional Guidance Scale, I was able to keep my emotions in check and approach the situation with a more positive mindset. I left the meeting feeling proud of myself for handling it so well and for not letting my emotions get the best of me.

Since then, I have continued using the Emotional Guidance Scale to manage my emotions and focus on the positive. It has helped me to become more self-aware and to recognize when I am slipping into negative thought patterns. And best of all, it has helped me to cultivate a more positive and joyful outlook on life.

Let's play *What If* for a moment. What if there is more to life than just existing? What if there is a bigger plan? What if, when you were a soul awaiting your birth into the human experience, you formed a plan? Your earthly existence is no accident. It wasn't born from random thought: *'I've got nothing to do for a while, so I think I might pop down to earth for a few years.'* You are here for a reason. You are a soul connected to Source and one that grows, learns, and evolves on this journey if it desires to do so.

I always like to have a visual of two umbrellas in my mind when I'm identifying an emotion. Those two umbrellas are labeled Love or Fear. For me, everything from 'contentment' and above on the EGS falls under the Love umbrella as they are all derivatives of love. On the flip side, I place everything from 'boredom' down under the Fear umbrella, as they all stem from fear itself.

When I'm in an unwanted state, I know I must choose a better-serving emotion that falls under the Love umbrella. The Emotional Guidance Scale aims to identify which 'rung' you are sitting on at any given time. Are you on a lower rung, wishing to improve your emotional state? Then it's time to pivot to a higher vibrating level of mind chatter, which will alter your emotions, directing your actions, creating your outcome. Identify your current mind chatter which is producing the unwanted emotion. Apart from asking your higher self what she would do when you are in the midst of unwanted emotions, here are two fixes that also work for me:

1. Physiology can alter psychology, which is just a fancy way of saying to change your stance, posture, location, or room currently supporting your unwanted emotion. Get up, go outside, walk around, put on some music, move, jump, sing, and bring in a more positive mind chat, even if it's initially challenging.

2. Remember chapter four, *The Magic of Appreciation and Gratitude?* Grab a pen and paper, change your environment if you can, and get writing on all the things you can appreciate right now.

You will know when you are not choosing, being, or doing your authentic or core self. Your EGS will produce feelings that we may deem *negative*, perhaps frustration, anger, jealousy, or resentment. This is not your authentic state. As you are a spiritual being currently having a human experience, joy and a higher vibrating way of being is your natural state. By the same token, you will know when you are choosing, being, or doing your authentic self because your EGS will produce feelings that we may deem *positive*, perhaps joy, a buzz, calm, happiness, peace or motivation.

Can you think back and associate times when your EGS has been at either end of the scale? Tapping into your Emotional Guidance Scale gives you a clear signal if and when you are off track. This forms the basis of the first self-inventory step in this chapter because it indicates something in your life needs changing, whether a little tweak or perhaps a major overhaul! From this awareness, you can then move on to the next self-inventory steps that we will be looking at in Part 2.

Awareness and acknowledgment of your EGS are crucial to move forward. I'm wondering, how many times have you dismissed feelings that have been lingering? What has been the outcome? Have these feelings magically disappeared, or have you had to or been forced to take action on them? So, how do you determine what your EGS has to say?

How would you rank yourself on the Emotional Guidance Scale today? You may have figured out that you're not exactly where you desire to be at present. However, it is important to note that all human emotions are beneficial, and each will be an important ingredient for growth. All emotions support a holistic human existence.

So, as your EGS lets you know which emotion you're currently doing, aim to acknowledge and understand what doesn't suit you and why, before you aim for a higher vibrating emotional state. Remember, with awareness comes knowledge, with knowledge comes wisdom, and with wisdom comes personal power. There may be an item of awareness in this current emotional state that you need to metaphorically pick up, try on for size, and wear around for a little while. It may not feel great on you, but by wearing it, you'll come to understand where it doesn't fit and what it can teach you about the outfit you should be wearing instead.

Your Next Steps:

Answer the following questions.

1. What encompasses my version of joy? (I really want to be experiencing this!)

2. What do I feel when I am indifferent? (I'll take it or leave it, I'm not fussed.)

3. How do I know when I'm experiencing fear-based emotions? (I really don't want to be experiencing this!)

So, you've now determined what joy means for you personally and how you define joy's opposite (fear-based emotions). Close your eyes and take three deep breaths. Connect with your higher self; this is done via thought. Ask *'What do I need to know right now?* Allow images, thoughts, sounds, or words to come to mind. Write down your received information. Remember, there is no right or wrong, do this exercise without judgment.

Chapter 7
The Belief Cycle

Belief is a cycle that begins with a thought, is fueled by emotion, and is strengthened through experience. It is up to us to choose which beliefs we feed and which ones we starve, for they shape not only our perception of reality but also the reality we create.

Believe it, and you'll think it. Think it, and you'll feel it, feel it, and you'll act upon it. Act, and you will have it. Your Beliefs Shape Your Life. What you see is who you are, and who you are is a product of your beliefs, your environment, your upbringing, your values, your needs, your community, culture, your past, your challenges, achievements, and most of all, you are a product of the level of ability you have to love yourself.

Your ability to love yourself is vital in shaping your overall development and personal growth. It influences how you perceive and interact with the world, impacting your relationships, choices, and well-being. Embracing self-love, acceptance, and compassion directly affects your self-esteem, resilience, and ability to overcome obstacles. By cultivating a positive self-image and nurturing a healthy relationship with yourself, you become a product of the love and care you invest in your own well-being, laying a strong foundation for personal fulfillment and happiness.

There is nothing about you that is wrong. I'll repeat that – *there is nothing about you that is wrong.* Where you are, right now in life is purely the sum of what has come before. Today is the answer to the equation of your personal journey in life up until now. If you want a different answer, add or remove something from your current life experience. All of the above (your upbringing, values, needs, community, culture, the past, challenges, and achievements) shape who we are and, at times, can give us a limited view of ourselves, our life, and those in it. Who we are is a precursor to our perceptions, followed by our actions. We can be wearing the most fabulous outfit and accessories, but we see ourselves differently due to who we are, what we focus on, and the beliefs we are driven by.

Getting to know ourselves deeper allows us to embrace a more flexible and tolerant approach to life. There is *'our way'* and *'all ways.'* In this 'all ways', you can separate from your ego form and be the observer, as we discussed in our last chapter, and connect with your soul's limitless possibility. Flexibility and the practice of removing the soul from the human self to witness a bigger picture opens up more paths to follow and more chances of success. You are not limited to traveling on only one road that may be blocked due to 'mind works'; yes, that's a play on the term road works!

Let's talk about Beliefs. Beliefs are merely repetitive thoughts that have been thought over and over again. Your personal truth is a belief you have held for a long time. The only meaning something has is the meaning we place on it. Suppose we form beliefs based on who we are or who we have been. In that case, we can most definitely form beliefs around the part of us we wish to uncover and embrace, that future self version of ourselves that, if we stop for a moment, we can see clearly in our mind's eye. We can feel the tingles that emanate from our emotions.

It is your belief system that really is at the core of the level of success you will encounter in your life. At first, this might seem confrontational, but when you get comfortable with just how much power you have to create your current life, you will be determined to use that same power to create the life you want. But a change of your belief system is not reliant on outside circumstances, other people, or fate. Change of your belief system is an inside job, providing yourself with mind food that is nutritious self-chatter and natural joy enhancers.

As with any diet, you see results with commitment, positive choices, and daily action. You embrace a lifestyle change. It is no different with changing your belief cycle. It is an ongoing commitment until 'new' becomes 'normal' and you have adapted a different way of believing, and therefore a different way of thinking, feeling, and doing, which will then provide you with different outcomes and results.

Now, let's look at The Belief Cycle.

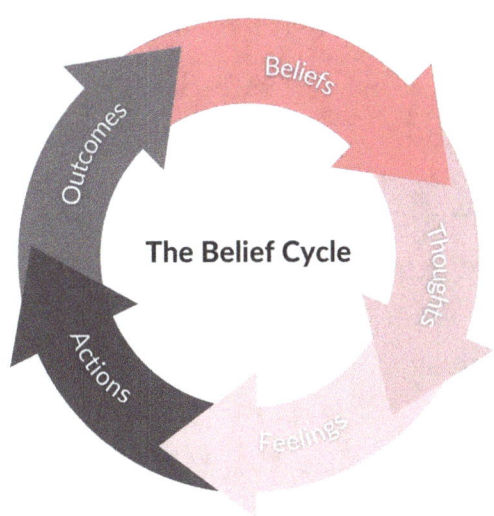

Your beliefs form your thoughts. Your thoughts produce your emotions, your emotions fuel your actions, and your actions provide you with results. All human behavior is running different strategies, running that belief cycle that produces outcomes. So what do you think could happen if you decided to alter a belief that doesn't result in a very good outcome? All beliefs end up in outcomes. You have so much power that is just patiently waiting until you make a choice to utilize it for a better life experience.

There is no such thing as failure. You will always get a result. *Always*. It may not be the result you hoped for, envisaged, or were working toward, but you always get a result. Disbelief gives you a result, and negative self-chatter gives you a result. Depressive feelings give you a result, and inaction gives you a result. So, for example, with 1 +1 +1 +1 +1, you get the result of 5. But what if you didn't want a five? What if you wanted a result of six? Then you would look at where in the equation you needed to change to get six. Example: 1+1+2+1+1=6. And this is the same with the belief cycle. If you are not getting the desired result, look at the five components in this cycle and ascertain where you need to adjust or modify personally. Discover the *chink in your chain*; what is happening in the strategy that is steering you away from your desired outcome, not driving you towards it? Is there a chink in your chain preventing you from your desired outcome? What could you alter for success? Understanding your chinks may show why you may have been stopping/starting on the journey toward joy.

When you can identify any chinks in your chain, any parts of the belief cycle that are detrimental to your desired outcome, you can choose first to alter or modify, then repeat, repeat, repeat, so that part of the equation becomes your new way of believing, thinking, feeling or doing to support your desired outcome.

Many of us use affirmations to create our reality. However, they may not be as useful if you have a belief, thought, feeling, or action that goes against what you want.

Some examples:

- *'Each day is a new opportunity!' However, deep down, I don't believe things can change.*

- *'I am my unique self!' But that doesn't win me many friends.*

- *'I love my body!' But I must do something about that cellulite before summer.*

You see, the 'but' negates the affirmation. It's diluting your belief in the statement. The gold is in the awareness that you gain from understanding your chinks. When you catch them, you stop the natural flow of an unhelpful belief, thought, emotion, or action. While its natural flow was once to infiltrate your emotions, actions, and outcomes, your awareness halts the energy of your current belief cycle and diminishes its power and purpose. Notice your chinks. Delete and replace them with a modified version. Why carry beliefs, thoughts, feelings, or actions with you that detract from your best self?

Helen's Story:

I used to be the type of person who would say affirmations every day. I would stand in front of the mirror and repeat phrases like, "I am confident," "I am worthy," and "I am loved." But deep down, I didn't really believe any of it. I was constantly filled with self-doubt and insecurity, and no matter how many times I repeated those positive phrases, I just couldn't shake the feeling that they weren't true. I tried everything to boost my self-confidence. I read self-help books, but nothing seemed to work. I was still stuck in a cycle of negative self-talk and self-doubt.

Then one day, I stumbled upon a new approach to affirmations. Instead of simply repeating positive phrases, I focused on why I didn't believe them in the first place. I realized my negative self-talk was deeply rooted in my past experiences and traumas. I had to address those issues before I could truly believe in myself.

So, I started writing down all the negative thoughts and beliefs holding me back. I dug deep into my past and uncovered the events that had shaped my self-image. And then I started to challenge those beliefs. I asked myself, "Is this true?" and "Does this belief serve me?"

Slowly but surely, I replaced those negative beliefs with positive ones. I began to see myself in a new light, and the affirmations started to feel more genuine. I no longer felt like I was faking it until I made it. I truly believed in myself and my abilities.

Now, when I stand in front of the mirror and say affirmations, I know they are true. I am confident, worthy, and loved, not because I'm just repeating those phrases, but because I've done the work.

Your Next Steps:

Answer the following questions:

1. Are you currently operating from a 'your way' or an 'all way' perspective?

2. If your answer is 'your way,' how might that prevent you from moving forward?

3. What other perspectives could you embrace right now that would provide you with a different life outcome?

4. What do you believe, think, feel, and do when it comes to deliberately creating your reality?

5. Do you recognize any personal chinks in the five parts of the Belief Cycle?

6. Consider the affirmations you like to use. Do any 'buts' feature? What undesired belief/s are they serving and supporting?

7. Even if the undesired belief/s once had a place in your life, does it really serve you now? Why not?

8. If awareness is the key to reworking neural pathways, what is one small thing you can do to alter any chinks in your belief cycle?

9. What steps can you take to optimize your belief cycle?

Chapter 8
Cause and Effect and the 5 Success Principles

Every cause has its effect; every effect has its cause. The universe is connected in a web of causation, and our actions and choices have the power to create a ripple effect that can shape the course of our lives and the world around us.

We now look at a wonderful reminder that further reinforces the need to analyze any beliefs that do not serve you. This powerful reminder is Cause and Effect. We tend to live our lives coming from one of two places, a place of 'cause,' or a place of 'effect.' With this explanation, you may see whether you or those close to you mostly come from cause or effect.

Living At Cause: When you choose to come from a place of cause, you know you are the driver of your own life.

Being at cause means that you know that you are the primary creator of your life journey and that, at any time, you can take responsibility, make choices, and explore other possibilities that are more appealing to you. You know that while you cannot control how another person chooses to live, you can make positive and rewarding choices for yourself. You take responsibility for communicating your choices to others. You have awareness and acceptance that others' choices may not be wrong, they are just unique to them.

Living From Effect: When you choose to come from a place of 'effect,' you believe it's someone else's responsibility to choose your life for you.

Being in effect means leaving your desired life up to chance, fate, or others. You don't tend to take responsibility, make choices or explore other possibilities that can change your outcomes to ones that appeal to you. You believe your life results from external forces, and you do not play a part in creating your desired life yourself. You may blame others or circumstances for your current situation or depend on others to find a solution for you. You may wait and hope for things to be different or others to provide for you. You feel life limits your options and blame external factors and others for your current life.

In summary, being at cause means taking control of your beliefs, thoughts, feelings, actions, and strategies in life to provide you with the desired outcome. You understand that although you cannot control others and outside circumstances, you can control how you react. Being in effect means you blame others or external sources for your life, your circumstances, your achievements, your mood, and your level of success. This places you in victimhood with the illusion that you lack choice in your life.

A point to remember: We are humans, not robots. Being human means encompassing all human states and emotions. Therefore, most of us will be living our lives weaving in and out of both cause and effect. The beauty of taking self-inventory and creating self-awareness is that you can identify when you choose to live in effect and recognize that it blocks the ease and flow of living in your joyous state.

So, why should you want to live at cause?

- It places you in the driver's seat of your life. You will get to where you want to go faster!

- It increases your sense of personal power. Do you mean I created that? You sure did!

- It proves that you are in more control than you may believe. No need to blame others!

The 5 Success Principles

The following 5 Success Principles will assist you in coming from a place of cause to achieve your goals or to take control of a situation.

1. Know Your Outcome

This is where creating a Smiley Goal will be put to good use. We will be looking at that in our next chapter. Knowing your outcome is equivalent to punching your desired destination into your GPS. You can plan the steps to get there when you know where you're heading. Being overwhelmed at the thought of 'new,' or 'change' generally comes from a lack of planning. In detailing your outcome, any undesired emotion will decrease, and you will have a clearer idea of where you are heading, what it will look like, how it will feel, and the benefits of working toward that goal. Knowing what you want will also highlight what you *don't want*, giving you a more streamlined route to your version of joy.

Whether you're planning a project or trying to achieve a personal goal, knowing the outcome can help you make better choices and take more efficient actions toward your objective. Without knowledge of the end result, you may waste valuable time and resources on actions that won't contribute to your success. Having clarity about the outcome you want to achieve can help you stay focused and motivated, leading to greater chances of success.

It can also help you manage expectations. When you clearly know what you want to achieve, you can set realistic expectations for yourself and others. This can prevent disappointment, frustration, and misunderstandings down the line.

2. Have Behavioral Flexibility

There are many ways to react to any given situation. However, most of us will react based on who we are, not necessarily what the actual situation is. We tend to react from habits, beliefs, values, needs, environment, upbringing, and character. This may bring positive or negative results, depending on the nature of the situation. I call these 'autopilot reactions' coming from an 'already always' perspective, which can be very limiting and do not provide us with the behavioral flexibility that can so often work in our favor. As mentioned previously, 'already/always' means that you are prepared to always react in a certain way. Behavioral flexibility allows us to step away from our ego self and witness a situation in its entirety (noticing *all ways*, not just *your way*), then make a choice to react or move forward in the most empowered and resourceful way for the best possible outcome.

This ability can bring a range of benefits, including:

Improved relationships: Behavioral flexibility allows you to adapt to the communication styles and preferences of others, making it easier to build rapport and trust. By adjusting your behavior to fit the situation, you can avoid conflicts and miscommunications that might arise if you are inflexible.

Increased resilience: Life is full of surprises and unexpected events, and having behavioral flexibility can help you adapt to changing circumstances and bounce back from setbacks. By switching gears and adjusting your responses to fit new situations, you can navigate challenges with more ease and confidence.

Greater creativity: Behavioral flexibility encourages an open-minded approach to problem-solving, which can lead to more innovative solutions. By being willing to try new approaches and adjust your behavior to fit new challenges, you can expand your thinking and come up with more creative solutions.

Better parenting: Parents who demonstrate behavioral flexibility can communicate better with their children. By being adaptable and responsive to the needs of your kids, you can enhance your relationship with them.

Overall, having behavioral flexibility can bring a range of benefits, helping you to build stronger relationships, navigate challenges with greater ease, and drive success in all areas of life.

3. Operate from a Physiology and Psychology of Excellence

Your physical body and your mind are a great partnership and will work together to bring you the success you desire or not. Both are not out to cause you to fail. However, by acknowledging the power they both have over each other, you can choose to think and conduct yourself in a way that will bring you closer to personal excellence.

Physiology creates psychology, and psychology creates physiology, meaning your body language affects your thoughts, and your thoughts affect your body language. Making changes to our psychology requires us to first look at our physiology. Our bodies and minds are intertwined, and when we change one, the other follows suit. To change our thought patterns and mental state, we must start by changing how we move or carry ourselves.

One of the best ways to do this is by practicing good posture. Our posture affects not only how others perceive us but also gives us a feeling of self-confidence and being grounded. Practicing good posture can help us become more aware of where we're at in the present moment and allow us to take a step back from any negative thoughts or emotions that may be coming up for us.

A powerful tool for improving our posture is to focus on lengthening our spine each day as we move through various activities such as sitting, standing, and walking. Not only will this help improve our physical health and well-being, but also positively impact how we feel mentally and emotionally each day.

In addition to focusing on posture, another great way to shift our mental state is by incorporating movement into our daily routine. Engaging in physical activity releases endorphins that can significantly reduce stress levels while creating a feeling of overall happiness, both essential for healthy mental states. Exercise can also provide an opportunity for relaxation, allowing us to take time away from worrying about day-to-day tasks or anxieties that may arise during certain moments in life. I don't know if this happens to you, but it's almost like a 'moving meditation' when I go for a walk. Because I've only got my mind for company and I'm detached from my regular activities, the walk seems to open a portal to those epiphanies that provide such clarity on a self-awareness level.

When trying to change our psychology through changing our physiology, it's important to pay attention to breathing patterns as well. Taking deep breaths can help regulate heart rate while slowing down the body's sympathetic nervous system response – reducing feelings of stress or anxiety while allowing for a sense of clarity and focus in the present moment. One powerful breathing exercise is called 'box breathing,' which involves taking four seconds to inhale deeply before holding your breath for four seconds, followed by another four seconds of exhaling before repeating the cycle once again, all while following a steady rhythm throughout the exercise.

Splashing cold water on our faces is another great way to change our psychology and reduce anxiety in the moment. Studies have found that this simple act can cause the brain to release endorphins, natural pain-relieving chemicals that enhance feelings of well-being. Cold water therapy also increases alertness and energy levels, which helps us become more focused and productive. It has been proven to lower heart rate and blood pressure, calming the mind and body in times of stress. Cold water also has a cooling effect on our skin, which can help reduce inflammation and relax tense muscles. Splashing it on your face helps awaken and invigorate your senses, preparing you for whatever task lies ahead.

Taking a few moments to perform this practice daily can help us develop better coping skills against emotional distress, such as nervousness or fear. Additionally, it's believed that cold showers can activate certain parts of our brains associated with pleasure and reward pathways, giving us an extra boost of relaxation. Overall, splashing cold water on our faces is an easy and effective way to soften anxious feelings at any given moment. Not only does it provide immediate relief from stress hormones like cortisol, but it may also help us better handle difficult emotions in the future.

Making changes to our psychology starts with looking at how we use our body as both an anchor point for grounding ourselves as well as a source of connection between mind and body – ultimately allowing us to create shifts in how we think and feel while finding balance within ourselves throughout various moments in life!

4. Take Action

Why action? Well, may I insert some simple logic here? If nothing changes, nothing changes.

Many small steps will eventually take you a long way. If coming from a place of cause means not counting only on external sources to provide, then taking personal action is the way to go. If you are one to freeze at the thought of the word 'action', you may be envisaging a leap instead of a step. Leaping is great for astronauts and if you personally have the resources and experience. In the meantime, stepping can meet the core needs of safety, security, comfort, and certainty and still take you toward your destination!

When you take action, you create momentum that propels you forward to what you desire. Each small step you take brings you closer to your outcome, building confidence and motivation along the way. By taking consistent action, you can create a personal positive feedback loop that drives your progress and helps you achieve your goals faster.

As you act, you may discover new insights and opportunities you wouldn't have otherwise found. This can help refine your approach and make more informed decisions about future steps. Because taking action requires a certain degree of courage and risk-taking, you build resilience and develop the ability to overcome setbacks and challenges. By facing your fears and taking action despite uncertainty or adversity, you become more resilient and better equipped to handle challenges.

5. Have Sensory Acuity

Sensory acuity is the ability to tap into your own senses, awareness, intelligence, and logic to detect whether a person, action, strategy, process, or indeed your self is working with you, against you, or not with you at all. It is sensing any tiny changes that indicate that an alternate approach in how you interact with someone or utilize something may be warranted.

For example, wine connoisseurs typically have heightened sensory understanding when it comes to tasting a variety of wines. They can distinguish subtle nuances in flavor that most people would not be able to recognize. Similarly, people with exceptional auditory acuity may be able to hear frequencies inaudible to others. Sensory acuity can also refer to the ability to pick up on nonverbal cues from our environment, such as body language or facial expressions. This type of emotional intelligence allows us to interpret the feelings and intentions of those around us more accurately.

For empty nesters, recognizing nuanced changes in their children's behavior may require heightened levels of sensory acuity. As children become more independent and self-sufficient, parents may need to pay close attention not only to their words but also to their actions if they are going to truly understand what is happening in their lives. High levels of sensory acuity can help parents feel connected even when their children have physically left the nest. Nonverbal communication can take many forms and is an incredibly powerful tool for expressing emotions, intentions, and meanings. Some of the most common nonverbal means of communication include eye contact, facial expressions, posture, gestures, personal space, tone of voice, touch, and body language.

Eye contact is one of the most powerful forms of nonverbal communication. It can express interest in a conversation or show agreement with someone's words. Eye contact can also imply disapproval or disagreement with someone's words. In some cultures, it is considered disrespectful to look someone in the eye while speaking to them, so it's important to be aware of cultural norms regarding interpersonal communication. Facial expressions are often used as a form of nonverbal communication. Smiles and frowns can indicate happiness or sadness, but even micro expressions such as raised eyebrows or furrowed brows can convey strong messages about how someone feels at any given moment. Posture is another effective form of nonverbal communication. Posture can range from standing tall and proud to slouching over with a defeated expression; both have different meanings easily recognizable by observers.

Similarly, body language such as crossed arms or twiddling fingers often conveys more than what verbal speech alone can communicate. The amount of personal space between two people may also indicate something about their relationship; if the distance between two people decreases during the conversation, it may signify growing intimacy. If the distance increases, it may suggest disinterest or discomfort with the topic being discussed. Another way we communicate nonverbally is through our tone of voice, which encompasses volume level and pitch variation along with certain vocal tics such as sighs or stutters that don't necessarily hold much meaning on their own yet still capture attention when heard in speech patterns. Touching someone on the shoulder or holding hands are both forms of physical contact that carry a deeper meaning than just a physical interaction; you both demonstrate comfortability beyond verbal speech capabilities.

Be aware to notice if what you are being or doing is moving you toward your desired goal and the results you desire. Watch out for the practice of 'busyness' without momentum. But, if you've known others who have been on a similar path that you are currently on and have gotten great results, please stick to your path; it may just take some more time. I have found that the more I invest in Self Inventory, the better sensory understanding I have for myself.

Anna's Story

I used to wake up each morning feeling tired and hopeless. I felt like I was stuck in a rut and couldn't find a way out. My low mood had been lingering for weeks, and I was starting to feel like it would never go away.

One day, while scrolling through social media, I found an article about the benefits of daily walks. It mentioned how 30 minutes of walking daily could improve your mood and overall well-being.

Feeling desperate, I decided to give it a try. The next morning, I put on my sneakers and walked outside. At first, I didn't feel any different. My mind was still consumed with negative thoughts, and I didn't think walking would make a difference.

But as I continued to walk, something changed. I started to appreciate the beauty around me, noticing the vibrant colors and the peacefulness of my surroundings. It was as if the act of walking had cleared my mind, allowing me to focus on the present moment.

Each day, I made it a point to walk, even if it was just for a few minutes. As I walked, I started to feel more energized and optimistic. I even started to look forward to my daily walks, as they provided a much-needed break from my negative thoughts.

Over time, my low mood started to lift. I no longer woke up feeling hopeless – instead, I felt motivated and ready to take on the day. Walking had become a part of my daily routine, and I couldn't imagine returning to my old habits.

Now, whenever I feel down, I know a walk can help. It's a simple yet powerful way to improve my mood and take care of myself. And for that, I am grateful.

Your Next Steps:

Answer the following questions:

1. Determine whether you are operating from a place of cause or effect. In which areas of your life may you not have been taking responsibility for your outcomes?

2. Who can you be to facilitate a more desired outcome?

3. What can you do to facilitate a more desired

outcome?

4. What is the first or next action step you can take toward creating a more desired life? Tap into your senses to determine what is working for you or against you.

5. Determine whether you are reacting to life from who you are or what life actually may be trying to show you.

6. Check your physiology (body language) and psychology (self-chatter/thoughts) to determine whether you operate from the point of personal excellence.

Chapter 9
SMILEY Goals

Set a goal that makes you smile, not just when you achieve it, but every step of the way. When your goal brings you joy, the journey toward it becomes a rewarding experience, and success is simply the icing on the cake.

So far in Part 2, we've looked at the Emotional Guidance Scale, we've looked at how your beliefs truly shape your reality, we've looked at how you can jump into the driver's seat of your life when you choose to come from a place of cause, and we've looked at five ways you can enhance your success.

When we do decide to drive our own life, in our own way, that is good for us and harmless to our world, well, we need a destination. Otherwise, we will feel lost and most likely give up on our journey as we don't have a clear direction ahead of us. In this chapter, I will introduce SMILEY Goals, designed by Graham King of the Australian Coaching Institute. If you think SMILEY goal setting might have been pertinent earlier on in your program, there's a reason I've left it until now. When it came time for you to write a goal, I wanted you to have a sense of possibility, hope, awareness, readiness, determination, and excitement around the task.

From the previous chapters, which hopefully have shown you how powerful you can be with more knowledge, tips, and resources in your toolkit, this is the perfect time to draft your desired destination. What differentiates SMILEY Goals from the SMART Goal-setting system we used in the decluttering chapter? Well, this goal inspired by your soul makes you smile from the center of your core.

SMILEY is an acronym for Specific, Measurable, Inspirational, Likely, Ecological, and Yours. Let's run through an explanation of each of the steps in the Smiley sequence of goal setting.

Specific

What exactly do you want to achieve? Be specific in detail about what you truly want because people who set specific goals are more likely to succeed.

Measurable

It must be measurable, meaning you must include a time and date or perhaps a certain amount, for example, the loss of 10 lbs by the first of a certain month and a certain year.

Inspirational

Your goal must be inspirational to you as it will help keep you motivated towards your finish line. We do not always have to achieve our goals alone; asking for help is a great way to get there. Although if your goal does not inspire you, how will you enroll others to help?

Likely

It's time for a reality check – is the goal you are setting achievable? The goal needs to be in your mind likely, achievable, and realistic for you. Any goal is possible to achieve, but you must believe it to be achievable for you, and is it likely to happen in the time frame set?

Ecological

The goal should be ecological, meaning good for you, the people around you, and the environment/planet.

Yours

And lastly and most importantly, is this goal yours, and Y (why) you want to achieve this goal? The goal cannot be for your partner, children, mother, father, or whoever else in your life you may be setting the goal for, you must be personally invested in the goal, and it must be for you.

An example of a SMILEY Goal:

Six months have passed, and I have successfully achieved my goal of giving up alcohol. I have created a healthier lifestyle by eliminating it from my daily routine and finding alternative ways to relax and unwind. I tracked my progress by journaling my alcohol-free days and noting any instances where I was tempted to drink but refrained. With the support of my family and friends, and access to resources and information on how to successfully give up alcohol, I achieved this goal. By giving up alcohol, I not only improved my physical health, mental clarity, and emotional well-being but also took a step toward a more responsible and conscientious lifestyle. I care deeply about my own health and well-being, as well as the health and safety of others around me. Living in a world where personal responsibility and community care are prioritized is important to me. By eliminating alcohol from my life, I aligned my actions with my values and am grateful to have made a positive impact on the world.

Let's dissect this goal and analyze how it meets the criteria of a SMILEY Goal:

Specific: The goal is specific as it clearly states that the objective is to give up alcohol.

Measurable: The goal is measurable because it mentions a time frame of six months and tracking progress through keeping a journal of alcohol-free days and instances of resisting temptation.

Inspirational: The goal is inspirational as it highlights the creation of a healthier lifestyle and the improvement of physical health, mental clarity, and emotional well-being. The support from family and friends, as well as access to resources and information, contributes to motivation and inspiration.

Likely: The goal appears to be realistic and achievable within the given time frame of six months. It acknowledges the presence of temptations and the need for support, indicating recognition of potential challenges.

Ecological: Although not explicitly stated, the goal to give up alcohol can contribute to an ecological aspect by promoting personal health and well-being, thereby fostering a healthier and safer community.

Yours: The goal is aligned with personal values and motivations. It emphasizes the importance of personal responsibility, community care, and the desire to make a positive impact on the world.

Josie's Story

I have always been goal-oriented, but recently I stumbled upon a new way of setting goals that has completely transformed how I approach them. It's called SMILEY, and let me tell you, it works wonders.

I decided to try this approach with a personal goal of mine: to run a half marathon. Using the SMILEY method, I began to break down my goal into smaller, more manageable pieces.

First, I made sure my goal was specific. I didn't just want to run a half marathon. I wanted to complete it in under two hours.

Next, I made sure my goal was measurable. I found a half marathon that was scheduled for six months from now and set a target pace of 9 minutes per mile. This way, I could track my progress and adjust as needed.

To make my goal inspirational, I visualized what it would feel like to cross the finish line in under two hours. I imagined my sense of accomplishment and pride and used that to motivate myself during my training.

I also made sure my goal was likely. I researched training plans and talked to other runners to ensure my goal was achievable with the right preparation and effort.

To make my goal ecological, I thought about how it would impact those around me. I knew that training for a half marathon would require a lot of time and energy, so I communicated my goal with my friends and family and found ways to involve them in my training when possible.

Finally, I made sure that my goal was truly mine. I didn't set this goal because someone else told me to or because it was the trendy thing to do. I set it because it was something I wanted to achieve for myself.

Finally, the day of the half-marathon arrived. I felt an overwhelming sense of pride and accomplishment as I crossed the finish line. I had achieved my SMILEY goal and done it on my terms.

Setting a SMILEY goal was the best decision I had made in a long time. It has given me direction, purpose, and motivation. And now that I had achieved my goal, I knew I could set even more for myself.

Your Next Steps:

Write your own SMILEY Goal!

Chapter 10
The 6 Core Human Needs

Understanding the six core human needs is essential to unlocking our potential for growth and fulfillment. They provide the framework for creating a life of purpose, meaning, and lasting happiness.

Humans have six core needs essential to overall well-being and personal satisfaction. These core needs are:

Love and Connection

Certainty

Significance

Variety

Growth

Contribution.

It is said that the needs of certainty, love and connection, significance, and variety are human needs, whereby growth and contribution are our soul's needs. Most of us will have one or two of these core needs that are more prevalent in our lives or more important to us. None is better than the other and each is based on who we are as people and our life experiences, encompassing things such as our beliefs, culture, religious persuasions, upbringing, schooling, environment, and the like. I was experiencing another *'my shower seems to be a portal to juicy tidbits from spirit'* a while ago as I embarked on my quest to serve empty nest moms. My mind went to the six core human needs. When I think about them, I always see these core needs having their own individual 'buckets'. It occurred to me that mothering, for a lot of us, fills all those core needs, those buckets, despite whether one or two are more important to us than another. I will explain what I mean.

Let's start with the core need of **Love and Connection**. If we are blessed, this core need is front and center of family life. Families are intertwined by love, shared DNA, experiences, shared interests, and family goals.

Now we move on to **Certainty**. We often have a lot of certainties provided to us as moms. We have routines within our day-to-day activities and can assume how most days will go. We have a home with a partner and kids, or perhaps with mom and kids. We are aware of what creates a good day and what creates a not-so-great day. We do what we do, and we know what we know, which can provide us with security and a level of comfort.

Next up, we have the core need of **Significance**. Well, I'm pretty sure that you, or you and your partner, were the most significant person in your child's life from day one. They relied on you for everything, whether for sustenance, nourishment, warmth, comfort, education, information, direction, or protection. You were the 'it' girl from when they were born, and for a lot of us, that reliance on us to provide for them lasted until they left home, and maybe still does.

Next, we have the core need for **Variety**. While there was a lot of certainty in the day-to-day happenings of raising children, there was also a lot of variety thrown in. From the different activities the kids participated in, to challenges such as illness, school happenings, family trips to different destinations, new needs that would arise, and even new hormones to navigate!

We then move on to the core need of **Growth**. Am I right in guessing that you are not the same woman you were before you had kids? I certainly am not. As my children grew, so did I, not only in the capacity to love another human being, but it was also an education, a steep learning curve in being all I could be to get this parenting gig right. Did I get it right all the time? Absolutely not, but as I always say to my girls, let some experiences of me as your mom be a great example and other experiences a horrible warning! We have a bit of a laugh with that one.

The last core need is **Contribution**. You brought a human into the world for a purpose. We all have one, whether that is acknowledged or not. You educated, cared for, and protected another human so they would grow and go out into the world to share their uniqueness with others in various ways. You contributed!

So parenting, for many of us, will tick all the core needs, or at least most of them. We go through the first 18 years of mothering with our core need buckets filled. And then, one day, when we pack them up, wish them well, and wave goodbye, those bucket levels drop significantly. Mom is gone when the kids walk out the door, and Remote Mom is born. She is a mom who still mothers, but from afar, in possibly quite a different way. I'm sorry... *What? What the heck just happened?* That is actually a response I got from a mom when I was researching the topic of empty nesting and how it affects us, and I totally get her.

In my view, this is the reason we as moms often suffer: we crash, and we are both shocked and traumatized when the children leave home. A sizable chunk of our life changes instantly, and we are often unprepared for the huge emotional and mental impact it will have on us. We lose our identity as we know it, we lose one of our life's purposes as we know it, we lose our day-to-day routine as we know it, we lose connection with our children as we know it, we lose our contribution to our children's lives as we know it, we lose social interactions that we once experienced because of the kids.

We are perhaps faced with the thought of not remembering who our partner is when he or she is not acting as dad or mom. It can often be jokingly like, *'I'm sorry, who are you, and what did you do with my partner?'* A significant contribution to our core needs has now gone. Crikey! Wow. Yeah. Now do you see why it's normal for you not to be in a great place right now? So much has been taken away—identity, purpose, interactions, connections, and routines, to name a few. Let's go back to the whole logical, life is made up of equations analogy. When we step back from our own emotions and view what has just happened to us from a place of being the observer, we can ask ourselves who are we *not to be challenged* to a certain degree when we become empty nesters?

Think of a cake and its ingredients that make it delicious, filling, and moreish. You have got flour, eggs, sugar, and fats at the very least. If we take away some or all those ingredients, you won't have the cake as you'd like. You have a bit of a mess on your hands. And this is what happens to us often as moms when the kids leave home and why we experience being a bit of a mess, like that cake. We are missing vital ingredients that made up our once-yummy life experience.

Does that help you be a little kinder and gentler when you find it challenging as an empty nester? If only someone had told me when I was nearing this phase of life, *'Hey Bobbi, just to let you know that the term 'empty nester' isn't necessarily referring to an empty home, it's because your core need buckets will become somewhat emptier from this experience. This is normal, and by referring to the six core human needs, you will have logical insight as to why it happened and how to have a full nest experience once again.'* Yeah, that would have been helpful!

So, how do we get those buckets back to a personal, desirable level? Well, let's go back to my signature system, the 3 As for Change, that forms the structure of your Post Nest Plan. We can apply those three As to the process of refilling those core need buckets. The first A, of course, is Acceptance. Aim to accept that your challenges right now may stem from a lack of one, two, or more of the six core needs being met. You are doing your best with the tools, knowledge, and resources you have had up until now.

The second A is Awareness. Look at each core need. Are there one or two that are of greater need or resonate more with you? How has your personal life experience altered from lack of each? How does this make you feel? What are the consequences of not currently having these needs met?

The third A is Action. Think of one thing, just one for now, that you can do to increase the level of just one bucket. Why one? One step forward today. One step forward tomorrow. After a while, many small steps have led a long way. What is one way you can now, as an empty nest mom, experience certainty, love and connection, significance, variety, growth, or contribution? It may not be in the same way you once experienced, and you may have to think outside the box, but it will be worth refilling to have a more fulfilled life.

Lastly on this topic, it is important to know one more thing. There are two ways in which we can fulfill these core needs – and that is either in a helpful or harmful way, to ourselves, those around us, or to the world. Let's look at empty nest moms and an example of Significance, along with a harmful and helpful way to achieve that core need.

Heather's Story:

When Olivia went to college, Heather lost how her core need of significance was met. She had two choices.

The unhelpful way she could have that core need met is by driving three hours and turning up to Olivia's dorm unannounced, offering her baked goods, tidying up her room, and doing her washing. She would have been holding on to the past way she experienced having this core need met, which was neither good for Olivia nor good for Heather.

On the flip side, the helpful way Heather could have this core need of significance met was by working part-time at the local elementary school in the canteen, providing little people with a nourishing meal, and becoming an integral part of her local school community. This would be good for her and those around her. Her need for significance would be met in a helpful way.

Just to let you know, Heather chose the helpful option!

So, when you now embark on looking more closely at the six core human needs and which is more important to you than another, I ask you not only to decipher the different way or ways you can now have these needs met, but I implore you also to consider how you can meet these needs in a way that is good for you, and also good for those close by and the world around you.

Your Next Steps:

1. Which core needs resonate more with you than any of the others?

2. Thinking of your *top two core needs*, answer the following:

- How were those core needs filled when you were in-person parenting?

- How has your personal life experience altered from lack of each?

- What are the consequences of not currently having these needs met?

- What can you do to increase the level of just one core need?

Chapter 11

Know Your Values

Knowing your values is like having a compass that guides you toward a life of authenticity, fulfillment, and inner peace. When you honor your values, you honor your true self.

Knowing your values is incredibly important in empty nest parenting, as this phase of life requires a shift in how parents relate to their children and vice versa. By understanding your core values, you can better understand what is most important to you when navigating this new family dynamic. This understanding can help you decide how to structure the empty nest relationship with your children to ensure that both sides are fulfilled and respected. Exploring personal values also helps you reflect on what you want out of life now.

Your values can change as you get older and your circumstances change. Knowing your values can act as a sort of compass, guiding you towards activities, experiences, and relationships that align with your innermost beliefs and desires. Whether you want to travel more often or spend time with other people who share similar interests, exploring personal values is one way to gain clarity on what you genuinely want out of life. Knowing your own values within an empty nest setting also allows parents to set healthy boundaries with their adult children. For example, if staying connected is a value for a parent but so is giving their children independence and space to grow, then establishing expectations around these two things can be a way for the parent to stay true to themselves while also honoring what the child needs from them. Knowing your values helps parents ensure that all parties involved are respected during this transition period.

Knowing your personal values starts with self-reflection. Ask yourself questions such as:

What is most important to me in life?

What kind of relationships do I want in my empty nest life?

These types of questions can help you identify what matters most to you, which can inform your decisions in your new life. Additionally, talking through these ideas with friends and family who know you well can be a wonderful way to clarify your core values.

Taking some time to explore activities and experiences that align with your interests is also an effective way to better understand what matters most to you and how those values might shape this new phase. Knowing your values can help you make more informed decisions when it comes to how you wish to live life now. Understanding what is most important to you can give you a better sense of direction when making decisions about relationships with your children, as well as how you want to structure life. Understanding your values can also guide you towards activities and experiences that align with your interests and beliefs, allowing you to gain clarity on what you want out of an empty nest life.

In short, knowing your values helps make decisions that best reflect who you are while honoring the needs of everyone involved in this change process.

Some examples of core values include honesty, integrity, respect, loyalty, family, hard work, humility, compassion, and empathy. These are some of the kinds of values that you may hold dear and strive to embody in relationships.

Honesty is being open and truthful with others — not withholding information or telling half-truths. Integrity is adhering to moral principles even when no one is watching. Respect means holding yourself and others in high regard and treating them with kindness and dignity. Loyalty implies faithfulness to oneself and those you love despite any changes or challenges that come your way. Family refers to cherishing the time spent with loved ones while standing by them through the highs and lows. Hard work is committing to achieving goals through dedication and effort over an extended period. Humility involves recognizing one's strengths and weaknesses without being boastful or prideful. Compassion entails understanding other people's struggles while offering support in whatever way possible. Empathy requires putting oneself in another's shoes to better understand their perspective without judgment. People often hold these values close to their heart as they transition into a new phase of life; these values help guide them toward making decisions that best reflect who they are while respecting the needs of everyone involved in the process.

Whether parents prioritize staying connected with their adult children or giving them independence and space for growth, knowing your values can help you make informed decisions about how to structure your new relationship style with your children. It can also help you explore activities, experiences, and relationships that better align with what matters most to you so that life can be a fulfilling experience for everyone involved.

Living by your values means making decisions that align with what you believe is important and reflecting on whether those decisions are true to yourself. This could mean setting healthy boundaries in relationships that respect everyone involved, committing to achieving goals through hard work and dedication, or cherishing the time spent with loved ones. It also means understanding other perspectives without judgment while offering support when needed.

When you come to know your values and gain a deeper understanding of what is important to you in life, it opens your eyes to the fact that your now adult children also have their own set of values. Just as you have your unique beliefs and principles, so do they. Recognizing and respecting their values is crucial for fostering harmonious, inclusive, and compassionate relationships. Understanding your own values allows you to appreciate the diversity of perspectives and beliefs that may exist within your family. It helps you realize that there isn't a single 'right' set of values, but rather a multitude of valid and meaningful ways each family member can navigate life. This realization promotes empathy, acceptance, and open-mindedness within a family. Respecting the values of your grown children means acknowledging their autonomy and allowing them the freedom to live according to their own beliefs. It involves refraining from judgment or imposing your values onto them. Instead, it entails actively listening, seeking to understand, and valuing their unique perspective. It doesn't mean that you have to compromise your own values, but rather find common ground and maintain a sense of respect amidst differences. By respecting the values of your children, you create an inclusive and supportive family environment where everyone feels valued for who they are.

It's important to maintain an open mind and approach each situation with respect and understanding when relating to your children's different values. Aim to see things from their perspective, ask questions about their beliefs, and be willing to listen without judgment or criticism. Most importantly, build bridges that foster mutual understanding by finding common ground while respecting their differences. Everyone is unique and has their own morals and values; being mindful when interacting with your children helps ensure that everyone is treated with respect regardless of any disparities in beliefs.

When you have determined your top values, it is highly important to learn how you personally require experiencing those values. Let me explain. Two people might value spontaneity. Your idea of spontaneity is trying a new restaurant instead of going to your regular one on a Saturday night. Someone else's idea of spontaneity may be deciding that a day of parachuting is in order. Do you see what I mean? Yes, it's helpful to know your values, but even better to understand how you wish to experience those values, what encompasses them, and what boundaries or limits you may have around them.

Another example is the value of socializing. My husband can do last-minute socializing, big crowd socializing, and staying up late socializing. Me? I love to get together with friends, but in smaller groups, knowing in advance and not staying out past about 10 pm. Knowing my values has really been a gift. A gift of certainty and perspective. The certainty that I'm making the right decisions. When it comes to decision-making and I'm unsure, I can think about my top values, the most important way for me to experience life, and see if saying yes or no will align with my values. A wider perspective helps me navigate and appreciate my children's differing values. This is not always easy, but it's beneficial for both parties and creates less stress for me and more harmonious relationships with both of them.

In a world of uncertainty, knowing your values enables you to stand firm and tall in your decisions. If your decisions harm none and are aligned with who you are at the core – perfect!

Avery's Story:

As a mother, my life has always been centered around my children. I had dedicated my time and energy to raising them, which was a role that had defined me for so long. But as my children grew older and eventually left the nest, I struggled to find purpose and meaning in my life.

For the first few months, I felt lost and unsure of what to do with my newfound free time. I had always been so focused on my role as a mother that I hadn't given much thought to what I truly valued. But as I started reflecting on my life, I realized that I had neglected my needs and desires for so long.

I started thinking about what brought me joy and fulfillment and realized that I deeply loved nature and the environment. I had always been passionate about protecting the planet but had never had the time to devote to it. With my children out of the house, I realized I finally had the opportunity to pursue my passion.

I started volunteering at a local environmental organization and became more involved in my community. I also started to make small changes in my life to reduce my environmental impact, like composting and using reusable bags and containers.

As I became more involved in environmental causes, I started to feel a sense of purpose and meaning in my life that I had never felt before. I realized that dedicating my time to something I was passionate about was the key to unlocking a fulfilling life.

I also started to focus on my own self-care and well-being. I started making time for hobbies I had put on hold while raising my children, like hiking. I started to prioritize my own needs and desires, which made me a happier and more fulfilled person.

Looking back, I realized that my empty nest had been a blessing in disguise. It forced me to reflect on my life and discover my true values. By pursuing my passion for the environment and prioritizing my own well-being, I found a sense of purpose and meaning that had eluded me for so long.

Your Next Steps:

It's time to determine your top five values! Remember, knowing your values will make life so much easier to navigate because it:

Provides Clarity: Understanding your values brings clarity to your life, helping you gain a deeper understanding of what truly matters to you.

Aligns Your Decisions: Knowing your values enables you to align your decisions and actions with your authentic self, leading to a more fulfilling and purpose-driven life.

Enhances Self-Awareness: Exploring your values promotes self-awareness by uncovering your deepest desires, aspirations, and beliefs.

Guides Decision-Making: Values serve as a compass in decision-making, helping you navigate complex choices and find the path that resonates with your true self.

Establishes Boundaries: Your values help you establish healthy boundaries in relationships, ensuring that your needs and values are respected while honoring the autonomy of others.

Enhances Communication: Understanding your values facilitates effective communication, as you can express your needs and expectations more clearly to others.

Fosters Authentic Relationships: Knowing your values allows you to build authentic connections with others who share similar beliefs, fostering deeper and more meaningful relationships.

Promotes Personal Growth: When you align with your values, you continually evolve and grow, pursuing goals and experiences that resonate with your true self.

Provides a Sense of Purpose: Knowing your values gives you a sense of purpose and direction in life, as you are guided by what truly matters to you.

Enhances Resilience: Understanding your values provides a solid foundation for resilience and navigating challenges. When faced with obstacles, you can draw upon your values to stay grounded and make decisions that align with your authentic self.

Here is a list of fifty values that may resonate with you. By all means, if one is missing, make sure you note it as one of your values!

1. Authenticity – being true to yourself and your values.

2. Balance – maintaining a healthy equilibrium between work, play, and personal life.

3. Creativity – thinking and expressing yourself in innovative and original ways.

4. Curiosity – a thirst for knowledge and understanding.

5. Dependability – being reliable and trustworthy in your commitments and obligations.

6. Discipline – having the self-control to stick to routines and schedules.

7. Empathy – understanding and caring about the experiences and feelings of others.

8. Excellence – striving for the highest quality in your work and accomplishments.

9. Fairness – treating others justly and equitably.

10. Flexibility – being adaptable and willing to change course as needed.

11. Freedom – valuing individual liberty and independence.

12. Friendship – building and maintaining strong, meaningful relationships with others.

13. Gratitude – appreciating and expressing thanks for the good things in life.

14. Happiness – prioritizing joy and contentment in your life.

15. Health – prioritizing physical and mental well-being.

16. Honesty – being truthful and transparent in all interactions.

17. Humility – recognizing and accepting your limitations and imperfections.

18. Independence – self-reliance, and self-sufficiency.

19. Innovation – seeking out new and better ways to do things.

20. Integrity – upholding moral and ethical principles.

21. Introspection – engaging in self-reflection and self-analysis.

22. Kindness – showing compassion and generosity to others.

23. Learning – pursuing knowledge and intellectual growth.

24. Love – valuing and prioritizing emotional connections with others.

25. Loyalty – standing by and supporting those whom you care about.

26. Open-mindedness – being receptive to new ideas and perspectives.

27. Optimism – maintaining a positive outlook on life.

28. Patience – having the ability to wait calmly and perseveringly.

29. Peace – prioritizing tranquility and harmony in your life.

30. Perseverance – persisting in the face of difficulty or obstacles.

31. Personal growth – striving to improve yourself in various aspects of life.

32. Privacy – valuing and protecting your personal space and boundaries.

33. Quality – prioritizing excellence and high standards in your work and accomplishments.

34. Reliability – consistently delivering on your promises and commitments.

35. Respect – treating others with dignity and consideration.

36. Responsibility – being accountable for your actions and choices.

37. Security – prioritizing safety and protection.

38. Self-expression – expressing yourself authentically and creatively.

39. Self-respect – valuing and prioritizing your worth and dignity.

40. Service – contributing to the greater good and helping others.

41. Simplicity – valuing a simple and uncomplicated lifestyle.

42. Spirituality – connecting with a higher power or purpose.

43. Success – achieving goals and fulfilling your potential.

44. Teamwork – working collaboratively with others towards common goals.

45. Trust – believing in and relying on the reliability of others.

46. Understanding – seeking to comprehend and empathize with others.

47. Uniqueness – celebrating and valuing your distinctiveness.

48. Wisdom – utilizing knowledge and experience to make wise decisions.

49. Work ethic – valuing hard work and diligence in your endeavors.

50. Zeal – pursuing your passions and interests with enthusiasm and energy.

Step 1: Reflect on Your Life Experiences

Think about the experiences that have shaped you into who you are today. Consider the positive and negative experiences and reflect on what you learned. These experiences can provide insight into your values.

Step 2: Consider What You Want in Life

Take some time to think about what you want in life. What are your goals and aspirations? What makes you happy? This can help you identify what you value most.

Step 3: Identify Your Core Values

Now it's time to identify your core values. These are the fundamental principles that guide your behavior and decisions. Start by brainstorming a list of values that resonate with you. Some examples include honesty, loyalty, respect, kindness, and ambition.

Step 4: Prioritize Your Values

Once you have a list of values, it's time to prioritize them. Start by grouping similar values. Then, rank each group from most important to least important. This will help you identify your top values.

Step 5: Pick Your Top 5 Values

Finally, it's time to pick your top five values. These values are most important to you and will guide your decisions and actions in life. Take time to reflect on your ranked list and pick the top five values that resonate most with you.

Step 6: Live According to Your Values

Now that you have identified your top five values, it's time to start living according to them. Make sure your decisions and actions align with your values. This will help you live a more fulfilling and purposeful life.

Answer the following for even more clarity on your values:

1. Values tend to change as we pass through different stages of life. For example, what a teenager values is usually very different from what a parent values. Think back to a different stage of your life. How were your values different? How are they the same?

2. Everyone has a personal set of values built from their unique life experiences. One crucial factor in what we value is the values of our friends, families, and society. How do your values differ from your friends and family? How do they differ from the society you live in?

3. Think of a person who you respect or look up to. What do you think their most important values might be? What strengths or qualities do they have that you admire?

4. We can learn a lot about our values by how we react to other people. Think of behaviors that you disapprove of or dislike from others. What does this tell you about your values? How would you behave differently if you were in their position?

5. Think of a value you have now that you did not use to have or has become more important to you. What life experiences led to this value change? How does this change affect you now?

6. The values we hold do not always align with our actions. Some values are difficult to live up to, or other priorities get in the way. Which of these values do you hope to focus on in the future? What life changes would you need to make to accomplish this?

7. How our values are shown differs from setting to setting. For example, your family might see a different side of you than friends, co-workers, or an authority figure. Think of three people from different parts of your life. How do you think each of them would describe your values? What evidence do they have?

Part 3: Action

Chapter 12

Parenting to Purpose

Soft skills are the building blocks of success. They are the glue that holds relationships together, the key to effective communication, and the foundation of personal and professional growth. With strong soft skills, one can navigate any area of life with confidence and grace.

This chapter is about affirming why it's your time to shine now that you're in this empty nest phase. The only thing that may be holding you back currently is your personal beliefs about yourself, life, or others, and even your imagination. How can I be so sure of this? Well, you have been in school for the eighteen-plus years that you raised children. You have been learning about, and putting into practice, an amazing skill set which I will discuss in this chapter. This may have gone unnoticed by you, but it has still happened. I bet you didn't know that you're an expert in soft skills, did you? I'll explain further.

An empty nest can be a difficult transition for many parents. It marks the end of a long journey of raising and caring for children, which can leave moms feeling lost and unsure of what to do next. From the research that I have conducted with empty nest moms just like you, reoccurring responses come up such as *'I don't know what my purpose is,' 'I feel like I no longer have an identity,' 'I feel so disconnected from others,' 'I have nothing to offer,' 'I have no skills'* and *'I don't know what I'm supposed to do now.'*

However, there are ways you can transfer the skills you used while parenting to another area. Moms develop a wide range of soft skills throughout their parenting journey. From discipline to problem-solving and communication, these skills are invaluable when raising children and can easily transfer to another area of interest once the kids have left home.

Soft skills are the abilities and competencies that allow a person to interact effectively with coworkers, customers, employers, and teammates. These include problem-solving, communication, teamwork, leadership, interpersonal skills, time management, and creativity. Soft skills are key factors in ensuring success in any field of work as they can be applied across a wide range of different areas, whether in the workforce, running your own business, or being part of a team. Let's look individually at each of those soft skills.

First, we have **Problem-Solving**. This is one of the most important soft skills for any environment. It requires analyzing complex situations and developing solutions to address them. Working together with others towards a common goal also requires strong problem-solving capabilities. Collaboration with others can be difficult when there are disagreements or different perspectives on approaching a task. With this skill set, you can assess various bits of information and develop strategies that maximize efficiency while minimizing risks.

Mothers are often incredibly good problem-solvers because of their unique combination of empathy, intuition, and resourcefulness. Often, they must deal with multiple issues at once – both big and small – and know how to assess the facts quickly, draw on their emotional intelligence, and develop creative solutions.

Next, we have **Communication**. This is essential in any area as it allows people to convey their ideas clearly and concisely while understanding messages from others accurately. The ability to effectively communicate through verbal, written, or nonverbal means ensures that tasks are completed efficiently, and goals are achieved successfully. Effective communication skills also foster a culture of trust, which can help build relationships between people.

Mothers are incredibly good communicators for a variety of reasons. One of the most obvious attributes is their natural knack for empathy and understanding. Due to their maternal instincts, mothers have an innate ability to recognize and respond to the emotions of others, giving them profound insight into how to communicate effectively with their children and others.

Next, we have **Teamwork.** This is a soft skill that involves collaborating effectively with others toward a shared goal or objective. It includes the ability to communicate, cooperate, and coordinate efforts within a group. Teamwork involves actively listening to others, respecting perspectives, and contributing to the collective effort. It requires setting aside personal ego and focusing on collective success, valuing the strengths and contributions of each person. Effective teamwork promotes trust, open communication, and a supportive environment where everyone feels valued and motivated to perform at their best. It not only enhances overall productivity but also cultivates a sense of camaraderie, achievement, and shared responsibility. This is paramount for achieving objectives as it allows people to leverage each other's knowledge and experience while building a sense of unity within a team. It enables people to divide tasks according to strengths and weaknesses so that everyone contributes something unique toward accomplishing goals more quickly than could be done alone.

Mothers are well-versed in the art of teamwork because they have the experience, intuition, and patience to be effective team players. From managing multiple children to juggling family responsibilities, mothers understand the importance of working together towards a common goal. They realize that collaboration is often required to achieve success and balanced outcomes.

Next, we have **Leadership**. This is another important attribute for contributing positively to any environment by creating an atmosphere where others are motivated and inspired to achieve their goals with passion and dedication. This requires excellent delegation abilities and effective decision-making skills so that tasks get done efficiently without sacrificing quality or creating too much stress for others involved with completing them. Leadership qualities also include inspiring commitment from others, which helps increase satisfaction levels among teammates, resulting in improved results.

Mothers possess a unique combination of qualities that make them excellent leaders. Not only are they compassionate and understanding, but they are also strong and resilient in the face of adversity. This strength provides guidance, support, and direction to those who most need it.

Next, we have **Interpersonal skills**. This involves interacting appropriately with people you come into contact with, whether they be customers, colleagues, or superiors while respecting their feelings at all times, regardless of differences or disagreements between the parties concerned. This important soft skill enables people to collaborate more easily, resulting in smoother workflow processes throughout daily activities inside any organization.

Mothers typically possess strong interpersonal skills due to the very nature of their roles. For example, they must be able to effectively communicate with children to provide guidance and nurture them through all stages of

No matter what your chosen path is now that you are an empty nester, soft skills will always be important. They are essential for interacting with others and managing your own empty nest interests. They are imperative in achieving success because they enable you to perform and better understand others' needs, solve problems collaboratively, lead fellow teammates, manage time effectively, and foster creative ideas. All these traits are invaluable in the workplace, in a community group, or in a volunteer role. Having strong soft skills will propel you in your chosen activities.

Most people can be taught hard skills, which are technical skills required for a job. The soft skills that you have developed over at least eighteen years of parenting are valuable and sought after. Moms possess many skills that can be easily transferred into the workplace, volunteer place, or hobby. One of the most important is multitasking. This involves managing several tasks simultaneously, often with very little time between them. We are often experts in this field, as we're used to juggling various tasks and responsibilities throughout the day, such as dinner preparation, bedtime routines, and managing children's school schedules. We have learned how to prioritize tasks and efficiently allocate our time to ensure everything runs smoothly.

Another invaluable quality we have as mothers is attention to detail. As moms must pay close attention to their children's needs and activities on a day-to-day basis, we develop a keen eye for detail that can be highly beneficial in any environment, whether professional or personal. From checking your child's homework to ensuring they complete tasks on time, we are adept at paying attention to even the smallest details when tackling any task.

In addition, mothers have excellent interpersonal skills. Having raised children requires a great deal of patience and understanding from both adults and children alike; these qualities help mothers communicate effectively and demonstrate empathy towards others when needed. We often master problem-solving; this includes both coming up with creative solutions in difficult situations and being resilient enough to remain calm under pressure when unexpected complications arise.

Overall, good parenting relies heavily on strong soft skills, making it an ideal foundation for excelling at whatever you choose to do once empty nest life appears. Mothers who move forward into something new, equipped with these necessary traits, often find themselves successful in their new roles thanks to their experience raising their own families at home; from multitasking abilities, attention to detail, and strong interpersonal skills – all these qualities combined prove essential for any mother wishing to establish herself outside of her family life.

I hope that by reading this, you have come to realize that you have so much to offer the world as an empty nester. This is not the end but the opportunity for a wonderful new beginning. Remember, whatever you do in this phase of life, whether it be joining a community group, establishing a home-based business, immersing yourself in your passion or favorite hobby, or returning to the workforce – you are strong, resilient, and capable. You can do anything your mind can dream of!

Your Next Steps:

Think of personal examples of how you used your soft skills as a mom when your kids were still living at home. Write them down for future reference.

Chapter 13

Finding the Key

Clarity is not just about seeing things as they are but about understanding the essence of who we are. It is the light that illuminates our path, the compass that guides our journey, and the courage to embrace our truth.

In this chapter, we will be traveling back to look at how far you have come with your awareness and to affirm the unique and wonderful person you are so that you can move forward with confidence, clarity, and certainty.

We will look for key threads, keywords, and indicators of who you are and what you want in this new phase of life. First, let's return to the Future Self exercise you did in chapter one and recap the benefits of doing this. One of the great benefits of doing a future-self exercise is that it helps you to clarify your values and what truly matters in life. By looking at your life from a long-term perspective, you can identify goals, dreams, and aspirations that are meaningful to you and that have the potential to bring lasting happiness and fulfillment. This can enable you to be more purposeful in setting your priorities for the present moment, allowing you to invest time and energy into activities that matter.

Additionally, by taking part in a future-self exercise, you can gain a better understanding of yourself. Taking an honest look at where you want your life to go allows you to reflect on who you are right now, how far you have come, and what actions you need to take to reach your desired destination. This helps build self-awareness which can lead you towards making smarter decisions, ones that are more reflective of your true beliefs rather than ones driven by short-term gratification or fear.

Engaging in this kind of reflection can help improve motivation levels by providing an inspiring vision for the future and giving you something tangible to work towards. A sense of direction provides focus, allowing you to better prioritize your efforts to progress towards your goals and objectives. It also increases optimism – having an idea about what lies ahead makes it easier for you to stay committed even when faced with adversity or times of difficulty.

Participating in this exercise can increase your confidence levels by identifying areas where further growth is possible and providing evidence of any successes achieved so far in your empty nest journey. This can lead to improved resilience which helps strengthen character during moments of failure or setbacks; having knowledge about your capabilities allows you greater freedom when trying out new things without fear or hesitation. This ultimately leads you down paths you may not have explored previously, but that could be beneficial in achieving your long-term goals.

Next, let's look at a reminder of the benefits of creating your SMILEY Goal. Setting a goal can have numerous benefits, both personally and professionally. On a personal level, setting a goal can help increase self-awareness and understanding of what you want out of life. It can also improve your ability to plan for your empty nest future by providing direction, focus, motivation, and purpose. Being able to set and reach achievable goals is one of the most important life skills, as it teaches you how to break down challenges into manageable tasks that are achievable over a certain period.

Setting sound goals provides more than just motivation; it enhances our problem-solving skills by teaching us to think ahead and anticipate potential roadblocks or challenges before they arise. It helps us recognize our weaknesses and strengths, allowing us to adjust while remaining focused on our main objectives. With each goal you set, you learn something new about yourself or the process you are undertaking, which can be used in future endeavors. Having achievable goals also makes you feel accomplished and satisfied when you achieve; this sense of accomplishment can be incredibly powerful in terms of increasing your self-efficacy and inner confidence.

Feeling successful leads to higher levels of happiness which further energizes you to pursue further success – leading to an increased sense of well-being over time. My husband and children have noticed a remarkable change in my overall happiness since I created The Inspired Empty Nest and accomplished a couple of business goals that I set for myself. They have seen renewed enthusiasm and genuine joy within me as I pursue my passion to assist empty nest moms. I am no longer sitting in sadness, but instead, embracing a newfound sense of purpose and contentment. It makes me incredibly happy to know that I am no longer burdening them with my challenging emotional state, and instead, we can enjoy a more harmonious and joyful family unit.

Achieving goals also gives you more opportunities for growth because once one goal has been achieved, something else is always waiting around the corner that needs striving for. Goal setting is an extremely beneficial tool that allows you to take control over your life while providing you with direction; fostering creativity and innovation; helping you stay organized and motivated; teaching valuable lessons about problem-solving, planning, and staying focused; increasing self-awareness and improving self-confidence—all while helping you achieve your dreams!

How did you do with becoming familiar with your Values? Knowing and understanding your values is a critical part of living a life that is both meaningful and fulfilling. Personal values are deeply held beliefs about what is most important in life, shaping your attitude, behavior, and decisions. A strong understanding of personal values can provide numerous benefits, from greater self-awareness to improved decision-making.

This heightened awareness helps create more clarity in life, allowing you to confidently make decisions that will lead you toward your desired outcomes. Understanding personal values also motivates taking action toward goals or dreams. Knowing which areas are most important allows you to prioritize accordingly, ensuring the necessary steps are taken on the path toward success. Additionally, knowing your values can help cultivate discipline in goal setting; having an internal compass helps you stay on track with your objectives. It allows you to make evaluations based on your standards of right and wrong instead of relying solely on external sources or opinions.

In terms of decision-making, understanding personal values can be extremely useful when faced with difficult choices or dilemmas in life. Knowing what matters most provides a sense of direction when making difficult decisions; this helps avoid confusion or second-guessing yourself as it creates a clear criterion for deciding among various options or paths forward. Furthermore, having knowledge of your values ensures any decision will align with your moral compass and support your overall vision for the future. Ultimately, knowing your values is essential for leading a successful life full of purpose and meaning. It allows you to understand yourself better by providing insight into what matters most; this insight then guides your actions and decisions, leading you down the correct path while avoiding potential pitfalls that come along the way!

And remember when we looked at the Six Core Human Needs? Here's a recap of their benefits. Knowing your core needs is an essential part of living a meaningful and fulfilling life. Core needs are deeply held desires that reflect your core values, goals, and motivations for being successful. Understanding your core needs can provide numerous benefits to you, from greater self-awareness to improved decision-making.

By recognizing and understanding your core needs, you can gain insight into your empty nest identity, enabling you to make more informed decisions about your future in this new phase of life. Having this level of awareness also creates greater focus regarding goal setting and taking action toward those goals. Knowing what matters most lets you prioritize accordingly to stay on track with your objectives. Uncovering your core needs also helps cultivate discipline; having an internal compass allows you to evaluate decisions based on your own standards of success versus relying solely on others' opinions. In terms of decision-making, knowing your core needs can be extremely beneficial when making difficult choices. Knowing what drives you means identifying which options best align with those core needs, providing a sense of direction when confronted with tough choices or tradeoffs between competing interests.

Additionally, understanding what matters most ensures any decision made will support your overall vision for the future and remain consistent with your moral compass and personal beliefs. Recognizing and understanding your core needs can lead to greater happiness over time by allowing you to pursue activities that align with your deepest desires rather than wasting time on activities that do not contribute toward long-term satisfaction or fulfillment. Knowing yourself better allows you to capitalize on your strengths while also addressing weaknesses to maximize potential; this sets the stage for achieving sustained success throughout life's journey!

And then we looked at all the amazing Soft Skills you have from parenting. Let's recap their benefits. Not only does knowing your soft skills provide insight into your strengths, but it can also help to identify areas for improvement and growth.

It gives you greater clarity in approaching life's challenges and successes. It helps you recognize and understand your emotional intelligence, providing guidance when faced with difficult decisions or dilemmas. Knowing what kind of support you need and how best to interact with others allows you to achieve greater self-confidence, leading to improved interpersonal relationships. As a result, understanding your soft skills enables us to develop trustworthiness through positive communication and collaboration with others.

What's more, knowing your soft skills allows you to take ownership of your successes and failures — something that is essential for greater personal growth. Through increased understanding of yourself, you can develop effective strategies for dealing with difficult situations such as criticism or adversity while gaining a more holistic view of each situation to make better decisions moving forward. Furthermore, being mindful of your soft skills supports the ability to take risks without fear; this allows you to make bold decisions that otherwise may have been avoided due to anxiety or a lack of confidence. Recognizing and understanding your soft skills is essential for leading a successful life full of purpose and meaning. It provides direction when making tough choices while allowing you the freedom you need to explore various paths without fear or hesitation; this ultimately leads you down the path that is most aligned with your core values as well as your vision for the future!

Having a greater awareness and understanding of who we are can lead to developing more meaningful relationships. Having knowledge of your strengths and weaknesses gives you the confidence to take risks and explore new opportunities, allowing you to become more creative and innovative in your pursuits. You can build stronger connections with those around you by being better able to empathize with your feelings and experiences; this deepens relationships through active listening and provides an opportunity for mutual growth and learning.

It also allows you to make informed decisions that align with your core values. You can be mindful of how your own needs affect your choices and how they will affect the outcomes of any given situation. This allows you to create plans tailored to fit each unique situation, while also considering all the necessary factors before making any decisions. Having an understanding of yourself leads to increased self-esteem, which in turn builds greater resilience; this is beneficial when faced with the challenges that may come your way as an empty nest mom—both big and small—as you are better able to handle any setbacks or failures to continue pursuing your goals.

Additionally, knowing yourself helps you identify what type of support you need from others to build healthier relationships moving forward. A greater awareness and understanding of who you are provides greater clarity on what truly matters most in life. Being aware of your deepest desires allows you to prioritize activities that bring fulfillment rather than settling for mediocrity or wasting time on activities that leave you feeling unfulfilled. In this way, recognizing who you are can open doors for sustained levels of success throughout your empty nest journey!

So now we've taken your conscious mind back to the benefits of your self-awareness gained in Part 2. It's time to look at those key threads, keywords, and key indicators of who you are and what you want in this new phase of life. At the moment, your mind may be overloaded with new personal insights, revelations, and epiphanies.

It may figuratively be like your mind is an airport landing strip, and you have a bunch of planes circling the tarmac. It's now time to become your own Flight Controller and schedule those metaphorical planes (meaning all your insights) to land, one by one, by going back to the notes you've taken and bringing all your ideas about who you are and what you want into one clear and defined area. This will give you a better perspective of who you are and where you wish to go from here, as a woman who is honoring herself, her needs, and her desires, and ultimately honoring her post-nest path.

Your Next Steps:

1. The first task I would like you to do is to revisit your Future Self. Has your idea of your desired future changed as you've learned more about yourself, or is it still the same? If it has changed, if you now hold more belief and confidence in yourself, your life, and those in your world, please go back and modify your Future Self exercise.

2. Once that is done, include your values, your top two core human needs and how you define living those needs, and the soft skill strengths you indeed have from parenting into a notebook for reference.

3. After you have done that, I'd like you to 'automatically write' an I AM piece. An 'I am' piece simply starts with those two words. The words 'I am' are incredibly

powerful because they can be used to declare an intention, goal or belief. By simply saying "I am," you are claiming ownership of an attribute or quality (e.g. I am successful), affirming that it exists within you, and placing yourself in a position of power as the creator and director of your own empty nest journey. Additionally, these two words have been found to possess strong psychological effects; when used together, they invoke feelings of confidence and assurance that whatever follows is true and real for you. Ultimately, the power behind these two simple words allows people to claim their unique identity while striving towards personal growth with conviction and determination!

Chapter 14
Secret Success Statement

Being of service to others is not only a responsibility we have as human beings, but it is also the pathway to discovering our own purpose and fulfillment in life.

Before I get into my Secret Success Statement, I would like to share a story about when I moved from Australia to the United States and struggled with overwhelm, fear, and anxiety about starting a new role in a new workplace. When we moved here, my husband suggested I do 'something that makes me happy', whether paid or voluntary work. So, in my often *'wow, that's so random'* way of being, I decided to do something I had seen growing up on television and in movies that was uniquely American. I decided to learn how to drive a big, yellow school bus!

I had no real idea what I was getting myself into, but once again, I decided to work on thinking about all this entailed later. So, I got my Commercial Driver's License, trained for six weeks with a local school district, and was ready to start transporting little people to and from school. I thought this was a brilliant way to assimilate into my local community, get to know the town I live in, and keep busy at the same time. Fear around my decision came knocking when it was time to leave the comfort of my training group and jump behind that oversized wheel in that large vehicle and, while reading a route map, start navigating my way around an area that I was becoming accustomed to, but certainly did not know well yet.

All the 'what ifs?' came out to play one day before I started the job while I was having a coffee date with a lovely Aussie friend who also happens to be an ex-pat living in the same town as me.

- We did not have navigation on the bus. We had to rely on reading from a route sheet.

- We were most definitely not allowed to touch our phones, let alone use them for navigation. That was an automatic fire.

- We could not use earpieces to hear navigation, even if our phones were far away.

- I was not familiar with the area I was driving in.

- I was starting as a substitute driver, meaning I would most likely be driving different routes on different days at a moment's notice.

- For the school year, it is dark when we start our morning routes for at least the first thirty minutes. How was I going to see house numbers and children?

This all freaked me out, and there was divine guidance in meeting up with my Aussie friend that day. I had known her for a year at that stage, and her family saved my emotional self with their understanding of the headspace one can be in after moving halfway across the world. She told me a story about how her Pastor at church said people often get worked up over things they must do because they are thinking of themselves in the scenario. She went on to say if we come from a place of serving others, our whole attitude can be altered. And I thought about this, and she was right.

I thought, *'Instead of focusing on making mistakes when I venture out as a substitute bus driver at the end of this month, I'm going to change focus and look at it from a service perspective. These kids are relying on me to get them to school. A lot of them can't get to school any other way other than on my bus. The parents need me to do this safely. The school relies on me to get their students there for the day's learning. Without me being of service, this wouldn't happen for a busload of kids. Sure, I might be a minute or two off schedule, and I might have to spend longer at a stop understanding where my next stop is, but still, I will be giving these kids a service that they need, so time to get over myself and focus on them. You're not a robot Self, nor are other drivers. We are humans living life, and life happens every day. Sometimes being late happens to divinely stall you, but I've got to focus on the bigger picture. I've got to come from a place of being of service. I will not think about being late. I will remember I am a human doing her best possible job with the tools, resources, and knowledge she has, working alongside what life has to offer on that day. If I trust in that perspective and process, I'll be surprised at how much life will support me.'*

Coming from a place of being of service, my focus was taken away from my perceived problems and directed to how I could help others. I was reinvigorated to keep going. I got my act together, and I carried on. And you know what? Those two years that I drove the school bus were some of the happiest years of my life. *Being of service rocked!* And even now, as I type this, I have goosebumps thinking of the high vibrating joy state that I would be thrust into when around those gorgeous little ones. And I got a bit addicted to this service gig. It made me so happy being useful, being needed, and having a purpose that I wanted to give back some more! The kids and I named Bus 31 'The Kind Bus', and we would do all sorts of activities around kindness, from acknowledging kind students on the bus to running donation drives for those less fortunate in our town.

I will never downplay what being of service has done for my life, how I approach life, and the ongoing energetic gifts I receive from coming from this perspective. And it is in this chapter that I will ask you to consider being someone who is of service. Now, don't panic – being of service is anything that takes habitual focus away from current challenges and focuses on how you can help others. Being of service is simply a mindset and can be conducted:

- In your workplace

- In a volunteer role

- As part of your hobby

- By starting your own home-based business

- By following a passion

- By joining a community group.

Let me know if you can think of any other ways, but I'm sure you get the gist of it. Being of service is simply a mindset of *'how can I incorporate who I am, what I know, what my experience is, what I value, what my current needs are, what my skills are, and how I envision my desired life, and be of service to others at the same time?'* Maybe you're creative and could teach others. Maybe you're tech-savvy and could create a course or advise others. Maybe you're a great team player and could assist in a community group.

Maybe you could be a mentor in your workplace. Maybe you have a great reason to run a Facebook group and help others. Maybe you helped your own kids with their schoolwork and could tutor others. The sky is the limit with ideas, and your imagination only limits them. So, you've probably guessed by now that my Secret Success Statement is:

BE OF SERVICE.

And when I say that, I mean: Be of service in your own way, by your own means, that is good for you and harmless to your world. There is magic in being of service because it allows us to make meaningful connections with others, discover new interests and skills, and experience a sense of satisfaction and happiness.

Service can bring great joy and fulfillment by allowing you to tap into your potential while positively impacting both people and communities. Additionally, giving back from a place of genuine passion rather than obligation can often lead to more rewarding experiences than just helping for the sake of doing so. Ultimately, serving others is an invaluable way to embrace life's beauty by connecting with one another in truly magical ways! You can choose from a myriad of ways in which you can be of service. This is an incredibly rewarding experience that can bring unique benefits to those who are ready to make the commitment.

Not only does being of service give you a sense of purpose and meaning, but it can also provide a positive outlet for your focus, energy, and resources. By changing focus, you can nurture another worthwhile cause now that your child has left the nest. For starters, being of service allows you to make a positive impact in the world around you. This could include helping with charitable organizations, volunteering at local events, or joining forces with like-minded people around you to create meaningful change. By taking part in these efforts, you can build strong bonds with your community and feel connected to something larger than yourself. Additionally, this kind of work often involves developing skills and competencies that can open other growth areas, such as increased self-confidence or financial stability.

Another incredible benefit of being of service is the potential for spiritual growth and renewal. Through this process, you may discover new values and beliefs that help shape your life meaningfully. This could involve exploring different religious or spiritual practices, engaging in activities that support personal development, such as meditation or mindfulness exercises, or deepening relationships with family members and friends by actively serving their needs. All these experiences can lead to a greater sense of purpose, connection, peace, joy, and fulfillment.

Being of service also offers the possibility for lifelong learning opportunities. These could include honing your professional skills through education programs designed specifically for adult learners or hobbies that involve learning new skills, such as writing or photography. Additionally, many organizations offer educational programs surrounding social issues such as poverty alleviation or environmental preservation, providing valuable insights into how you can make positive changes in your world today.

Being of service as an empty nest mom offers significant rewards. Embracing this time in life is beneficial and necessary if you want to continue creating positive change in your community and beyond! You can find your niche in being of service by exploring the different options available to you. A great place to start is by connecting with local community organizations or charities and asking how you can help out. This may include volunteering for several hours weekly, helping at events, or even taking on a leadership role in their organization. Additionally, many non-profits offer free courses or workshops that provide valuable information on how to make a meaningful impact in the lives of others.

Creating your own venture can be a fulfilling and empowering path forward. Perhaps you could tap into your creative talents and launch a small craft business, sharing your unique creations with the world. You could leverage your knowledge and experience to become a consultant, offering your expertise in areas you excelled at while raising your children. You could delve into the digital realm, establishing an online presence through blogging, vlogging, or podcasting, allowing you to connect with a wide audience and share your insights on topics close to your heart. You can explore your entrepreneurial spirit by starting a home-based business, such as catering or interior design. With determination, passion, and a willingness to embrace new opportunities, you can create your own venture and embark on a fulfilling and rewarding next chapter of your life.

You could also investigate courses in subjects such as arts and culture, social justice, environmental sustainability, financial management, technology trends, and more – all of which can help expand your knowledge base and improve your skill set.

There are numerous ways for you to find your niche in being of service – from engaging with local organizations to developing your venture or connecting with like-minded people who share the same vision of making a positive impact on the world around you. Regardless of your chosen path, this kind of work is incredibly rewarding and provides unique benefits such as increased self-confidence and spiritual renewal through meaningful connections with others.

We can learn from people who came before us about serving others. Back in 2005, I was the manager of a Sydney Legacy branch in Australia. Legacy helps war widows financially, emotionally, and physically. I used to ponder the contented and happy nature of these women I would interact with daily. They came from a different time than me and had husbands mostly killed in combat or from combat-related afflictions in World War 2, Korea, or Vietnam. Like my grandmother, I realized that they were from an era where it was expected that they would serve others when times were challenging.

I saw that they carried on these traits of helpfulness, kindness, and generosity in their later years, and I remember always wondering why they were so happy. They had lost their husbands, were getting older, and were becoming more limited. But the ladies that showed up week after week had a purpose: to continue serving each other now that they were widowed.

You, too, can be of service by volunteering and helping with local organizations, starting your own businesses, or joining groups working on making the world a better place. You can also take classes to learn more about different topics so you can help others even more. Serving others is a great way to combat loneliness and help foster meaningful connections with those around us. Helping others gives you a sense of purpose which can be incredibly fulfilling in making you feel more connected to your community and loved ones. It is a 'lack of purpose' that comes up repeatedly as a current reality for empty nest moms. You can turn this around, I promise. Ultimately, being of service can make a positive impact in the world while allowing yourself to experience life's many joys.

When it comes to rediscovering your identity and being of service, several different strategies can be employed. The first step is to assess your soft and hard skills and passions and find areas where you can make the most meaningful impact. This could involve looking at what opportunities exist within the local community or researching various organizations and initiatives that align with your interests. For instance, someone passionate about helping the homeless population may decide to volunteer with a local shelter or arrange donation drives for the less fortunate in their area.

Similarly, someone who enjoys working with children may choose to become a mentor in an after-school program or even create their own youth-focused initiative. In this way, you can align your actions with your values and interests while contributing to the wider world. In addition, those who are dedicated to being of service may consider taking part in advocacy work related to the causes they care about most.

For example, if somebody is passionate about protecting the environment, then they could join groups or campaigns focused on environmental conservation or speak out about climate change issues through online platforms such as social media. A great way to connect with others who share similar interests is via the meetup.com app.

You can also look for ways to deepen your understanding of how you can contribute meaningfully by learning from those around you who have similar aspirations. One great way of doing this is by getting involved in professional networks, such as the American Business Women's Association. This could involve attending events like workshops and conferences that teach people how to be more effective in their volunteering roles or meeting up with experienced professionals who share tips on how these activities can bring positive change locally and globally. Discovering your empty nest identity when being of service requires you to reflect upon what inspires you most and look for opportunities to use your talents and resources for the greater good. You may also consider getting involved in advocacy work related to causes you believe in and seek learning opportunities from experienced professionals, so you know how best to help others in meaningful ways.

When you choose to focus your energy on serving others, it can take you out of a place of feeling powerless over your current empty nest challenges and give you a sense of purpose. By helping others, you are not only making their lives better but also improving your own well-being.

Serving others allows you to expand your horizons, gain new perspectives and knowledge, and even learn transferable skills that can be applied in the future. When you choose to help those who are less fortunate than you or who have experienced similar struggles as you have faced in the past, it offers great emotional satisfaction — you often find that there is a greater reward in helping another person than in striving for personal gain alone. I knew this to be true when I started The Inspired Empty Nest. From my background in human behavior, I had the tools and techniques I needed to help myself, however taking other moms along for this healing journey would be a more meaningful and rewarding experience.

Engaging in service-oriented activities like volunteering or advocating for causes close to your heart, or working with nonprofits or other organizations promoting positive change in society at large, allows you to lead meaningful lives with real impact. One of the most rewarding benefits of being of service is the feeling of personal fulfillment that comes with helping others.

When you contribute your time and energy to a service, cause, or group you are passionate about, you can make meaningful contributions to your community, regardless of your age or place. Beyond these tangible benefits, being of service can also help improve mental well-being in significant ways. Research has shown that giving back by being of service leads to increased happiness and overall satisfaction with life.

Studies suggest this boost may come from the sense of purpose, connection, and self-esteem that those who are of service experience when they can make positive changes in their community or environment. It can also relieve stress, allowing you to take your mind off your troubles and focus on helping others instead.

My passion for serving others and using my skills and abilities to make a difference in the world makes me happy. That doesn't mean I can do everything, but it does mean that I am always looking for ways to help those who are less fortunate than myself or who have experienced similar struggles. This may be offering support via coaching, sharing empty nest stories from moms on my Fly Mom, Fly! podcast, speaking at events, or providing a safe space in The Inspired Empty Nest Moms Group on Facebook. I take great joy in knowing that my efforts are impacting the lives of others, no matter how small. It gives me a sense of purpose and satisfaction that nothing else can match. Knowing I am doing something meaningful energizes me and motivates me to continue giving back even when times get tough.

When it comes to overcoming the fear of not having anything to offer the world, it is important to remind ourselves that everyone has something unique and special to contribute – no matter your age, gender, race, or background. Even small gestures of kindness and generosity can have a lasting impact on those around us. You never know how a small act you offer today may change someone's tomorrow.

One of the best ways to tap into this potential is by getting out of our comfort zone and exploring new service opportunities. Stepping outside of our routine can help widen our perspectives and open up new possibilities for how we might be able to help others. Rather than ignoring our doubts about not having anything to offer the world, we must take time to really consider our strengths and weaknesses with an open mind. We must recognize that any skills or attributes we may possess could be put toward making a positive difference in some way – even if it isn't as grand as we initially hoped.

Finding meaningful ways to give back doesn't necessarily involve money or tangible donations; sharing knowledge or providing emotional support are valuable contributions! When people feel connected with something larger than themselves through service-oriented activities, they often feel more satisfied with their lives. It is important to remember that what matters most is not necessarily how much you do but rather *how much you care about doing it* in the first place. Giving from a place of authenticity will always be more rewarding than giving just because you feel obligated or pressured by society. So let go of fears about not having anything valuable to offer the world and instead focus on what motivates you most deeply when deciding how you want to contribute!

Chapter 15
Motivating Me

Discovering your calling in life is not about finding something outside of yourself; it's about uncovering the unique purpose that already resides within you and committing to bringing it to life.

In the last chapter, we looked at being of service, a magical way to refocus from the grief, loss, disconnection, and loneliness many empty nesters face and toward purpose, direction, and fulfillment. Another way to understand your unique way of being of service is to identify which of the Ps drives you more.

The three Ps are Problem, Proficiency, or Passion. This chapter will help you consider which of the Ps resonates with you the most and, how that can help you find the best way to be of service. In this chapter, it is best to notice your heart space and any emotions that come with considering each of the Ps. *Your internal guidance system will let you know which path may be best for you.* Let's run through each P.

We'll start with someone who resonates as a **Problem Solver** or has a particular interest in an area that requires finding solutions. A problem solver is like a superhero who helps tackle challenges and find solutions. They have a set of unique attributes that make them great at what they do. First, they have a keen ability to observe and understand problems. They pay close attention to details and take the time to comprehend the situation at hand fully. Next, problem solvers are creative thinkers. They can come up with new and innovative ideas to solve problems, thinking outside the box when others might get stuck. They are also persistent and determined, never giving up easily. Even when faced with obstacles, they keep trying different approaches until they find the right solution.

Additionally, problem solvers are excellent communicators. They listen attentively to others' perspectives and ideas, and they can explain their own thoughts clearly. This helps them collaborate effectively with others to solve complex problems. Finally, problem solvers are adaptable. They can quickly adjust their strategies if the situation changes or new information arises. This flexibility allows them to navigate unexpected challenges with ease. With their observation skills, creativity, persistence, communication abilities, and adaptability, problem solvers are superheroes who can conquer any problem that comes their way.

My husband possesses an exceptional talent for problem-solving. While I often find myself grappling with the complexities of addressing issues, he effortlessly embraces the role of a problem solver in both his professional and personal life. As the president of a large manufacturing firm, he relishes the challenges that come with his demanding position, tackling the daily hurdles that arise within his workplace. Moreover, his dedication extends beyond the confines of his office. Serving on the Board of our neighborhood's Homeowners Association, he willingly embraces the influx of messages, complaints, and concerns from our 800 residents at any given time. When I questioned him after his first year on the Board, wondering if he would run for re-election considering the immense workload, his response was resolute: "Of course, I love fixing problems and helping people!"

Let's now look at **Proficiency.** Imagine someone who is like a master in their field and incredibly good at what they do. This person has a unique set of attributes that sets them apart. First, they have a deep knowledge and understanding of their craft. They have invested time and effort to gain expertise in their specialization, and they continue to learn and grow to stay at the top of their game. Secondly, they possess exceptional skills. Whether playing a musical instrument, cooking delicious meals, or building intricate structures, their skills are unmatched. They are highly focused and disciplined, able to concentrate on their work without getting easily distracted, allowing them to achieve outstanding results. Finally, they have a passion for what they do. Their love and enthusiasm for their craft fuel their motivation and drive, inspiring others around them.

Lastly, we now look at **Passion**. This person radiates enthusiasm and excitement whenever they engage in their chosen pursuit. They have an infectious and inspiring love for their work or hobby. One of the key attributes of someone with a passion for what they do is their dedication. They are fully committed to their craft, investing their time, energy, and effort wholeheartedly. They thrive in environments where they can share their passion and inspire others. Their genuine excitement and zest for their work uplift those around them, creating a motivating and encouraging atmosphere. Passion is at the core of my work with The Inspired Empty Nest.

Dawn's Story:

For the first time in over two decades, I was alone. My children had all flown the nest, and I was left with an empty house and an even emptier feeling inside. For years, my life had revolved around my children. I had put all my energy into raising them, putting my own dreams on hold. But now that they were gone, I felt lost and unsure of who I was outside of the role of "mom."

At first, I tried to fill the void with volunteer work and hobbies, but nothing seemed to bring me the fulfillment I craved. It wasn't until I started to look inward that I began to uncover my true passion. Reflecting on my life, I realized that I had always loved cooking and entertaining. I had always been the one to host holiday dinners and dinner parties for friends and family. Then, I realized that my passion lay in the culinary arts.

I enrolled in cooking classes and started experimenting with different recipes in my kitchen. I even started a blog to share my creations with others. As I dove deeper into my passion for cooking, I found that the emptiness I had been experiencing slowly faded away.

Cooking gave me a sense of purpose and fulfillment that I had never experienced before. I started hosting dinner parties again, but this time, it was different. I wasn't doing it to impress anyone or fulfill societal expectations of what a good hostess should be. I was doing it because I loved it.

Through cooking, I discovered my true calling in life. I had found something that filled the emptiness inside and gave me a sense of joy and purpose. I had finally found myself and knew I would never be lost again.

Your Next Steps:

Answer the following questions:

1. What am I most passionate about?

2. How can I use my current skills and abilities to make a difference in the world?

3. What do I feel is important enough to dedicate my time and energy towards?

4. Are there any causes that resonate with me on a deep level?

5. Am I open to new opportunities or taking risks when it's necessary for growth?

6. What do I want to accomplish in the near future?

7. Will this help me progress toward achieving my dreams?

8. Do I have a plan of action that will help me reach my goals?

9. Have I surrounded myself with people who will support and encourage me on this journey?

10. How can I challenge myself more effectively so that I am continually growing and learning new skills?

11. Are there any riskier activities or experiments that could help me gain perspective or improve a skill set quickly?

12. What activities make me feel most content?

13. How can I enjoy my free time more productively?

14. What things do I value deeply that add to my overall well-being?

15. Is there anything that brings out the best in me and others around me?

16. Are there any experiences or people who bring joy into my life regularly?

Chapter 16

Making a Choice

Making a choice is not just about deciding between options; it is about choosing the path that aligns with your values, reflects your integrity, and leads you toward your true purpose.

By this stage of your Post Nest Plan, you have come to know yourself so much more. You've learned the pain of remaining in the same space you were in when you started this book. You've discovered the excitement of your future self. You've understood the importance of first *being*, then *doing*, so you may *have*. You've had a glimpse of how life-changing appreciation and gratitude can be. You've learned how energy works and how to declutter your space to allow the new into your life. You value the importance of taking self-inventory. You've learned how your beliefs impact your life through the Belief Cycle. You now know the power of being at cause in your life rather than living at effect. You know the 5 Success Principles. You've set your GPS to happiness your way by creating a SMILEY Goal.

You've learned where your empty nest challenges may have come from through depleted core human needs buckets.

You came to understand your core values and how you define experiencing them. You learned the value of sensory acuity to know when things need modifying or aren't exactly right for you. You came to understand the awesome soft skills you developed from parenting. You know the magical effect being of service has on your life. You looked at whether you would be best suited in an environment of problem-solving, working at something you're proficient at, or following your passion. Maybe it's all three!

Wow! You have learned so much, and I am very proud of you! I know firsthand what it's like to go through the journey that is this book and, even more so, the personal growth that comes with it.

There is one more thing that I would like to share with you regarding being of service. Being of service can also mean being of service to yourself via a hobby or self-care routine. You may think that a bit odd. *Being of service to myself, Bobbi?* Yes! And do you know why it can be so beneficial? I'll explain.

Participating in an enjoyable hobby or indulging in self-care practices nourishes our mental, emotional, and physical well-being. Engaging in activities we love brings us joy, reduces stress, and promotes a sense of fulfillment. When we make time for ourselves, we recharge our batteries, regain balance, and improve our overall resilience. This renewed sense of well-being allows us to show up fully and wholeheartedly in our interactions with others, bringing our best selves to the table.

When we prioritize self-care and engage in activities that bring us joy, we raise our vibrational energy levels. As a pebble dropped into a pond, our positive energy ripples outwards, affecting everyone we encounter. Our uplifted spirit, optimism, and enthusiasm become contagious, spreading positivity to those around us. Whether it's our family, friends, colleagues, or even strangers, our positive energy can inspire, motivate, and uplift others, creating a ripple effect of positivity in the world.

Taking care of ourselves enables us to cultivate healthier relationships with others. When we meet our needs and prioritize self-care, we fill our cup, ensuring we have abundant love, compassion, and understanding to share. By nurturing ourselves, we develop a more profound sense of self-awareness and emotional intelligence, allowing us to empathize more effectively with others. Our increased capacity for empathy enables us to offer genuine support, listen attentively, and provide a safe space for others to express themselves authentically.

By prioritizing self-care, we set an example for others to follow. Our conscious commitment to personal well-being demonstrates the importance of self-nurturing and self-respect. Others are inspired to do the same when they witness our dedication to self-care. By embodying self-care practices, we advocate for personal growth and holistic well-being. Through our actions, we create a ripple effect that encourages others to prioritize their own needs, creating a community of people who are more balanced, fulfilled, and ready to positively impact the world. When thinking about being of service, it's crucial to remember that serving ourselves is not selfish but can be an act of profound service to the world around us.

Michelle's Story:

When my children left home, I felt like a piece of me had been ripped away. I had been a stay-at-home mom for 20 years and didn't know who I was outside of that role. I tried to fill the void by volunteering, taking classes, and going on trips, but nothing seemed to click.

One day, while organizing my closet, I realized I had a passion for decluttering and organization. I have always enjoyed finding new ways to maximize space and keep things tidy. So, I decided to turn my passion into a business.

I offered services such as closet organization, pantry organization, and home office organization. At first, I didn't have many clients, but I kept pushing forward. I offered free consultations and discounts to friends and family members, and they began to spread the word about my services. I also joined local Facebook groups and forums for moms and homeowners and shared my business with them.

As my client base grew, so did my confidence. I found that I had a talent for creating functional and beautiful spaces, and my clients were thrilled with the results. Not only was I providing a valuable service, but I was also making a difference in people's lives.

Starting my decluttering business gave me a sense of purpose and direction that I had been missing. It allowed me to use my skills and passion to help others and provided me with a source of income.

I never thought I could turn my love of organization into a successful business, but I did. And if you're feeling lost after your children leave home, I encourage you to find something you're passionate about and turn it into a business. You never know where it might take you.

Your Next Steps:

How do you feel you can be of service to yourself, your community, or the world as a whole? Remember, being of service to yourself in a way that does not harm is also beneficial, as the ripple effect from filling your own happy tank will alter not only your life but those around you as well.

Chapter 17
Your Post Nest Plan

Planning is not just about charting a course toward your goals; it is about taking control of your destiny, empowering yourself to navigate the unpredictable waters of life, and, ultimately, creating the future you desire.

Now is the time to compile your Post Nest Plan to rock the reignited you!

There are two ways to complete your Post Nest Plan:

Insert your compiled information from the activities in this book into the categories outlined:

- My Future Self Statement

- My Top 2 Core Needs

- My Top 5 Values

- My Top Soft Skills

- My SMILEY Goal

- Key Threads / Key Words / Key Indicators

- The P that Motivates Me

- My Service Format

- My Post Nest Plan Is

Or, should you be more visual and want a template of the Post Nest Plan to print and fill in, visit **inspiredemptynest.com** and find it under the **Resources** tab.

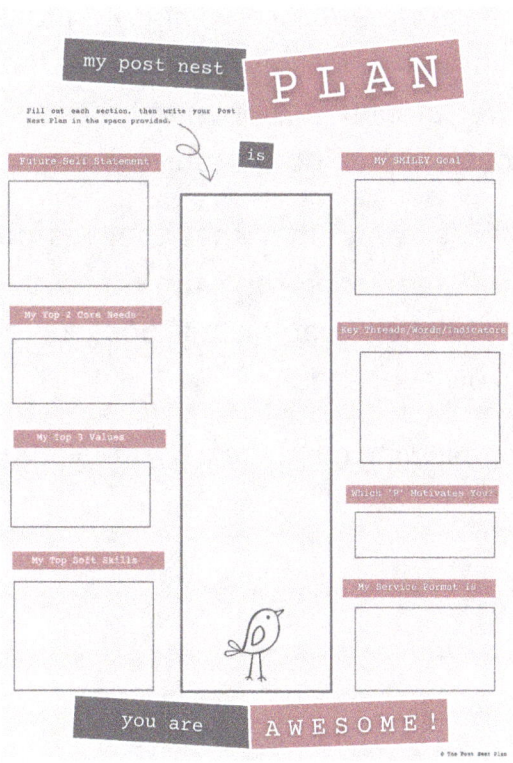

Thank you for joining me on this journey of self-discovery and reinvention. I hope The Post Nest Plan has inspired you to embrace the next chapter of your life enthusiastically and confidently. Life is a journey, and sometimes the path may seem unclear, but with determination and a positive mindset, you can create a fulfilling and meaningful future.

Please stay in touch and let me know about your own Post Nest Plan. I would love to hear your stories and share in your successes. Together, we can continue to support and encourage each other along the way.

If you find the time and are willing, I kindly ask you to consider leaving a review of my book on Amazon. Your words have the power to influence potential readers and make a significant impact on the book's journey.

However, please remember that there is absolutely no obligation to leave a review. Your support in any form, whether it's through reading my book or sharing your thoughts, is truly appreciated.

Thank you for allowing me to be a part of your journey.

Sincerely,

Bobbi Chegwyn.

About the Author

Since becoming an Advanced Practitioner of Life Coaching and Practitioner of Neuro Linguistic Programming with The Coaching Institute in Melbourne, Australia, in 2008, Bobbi has helped hundreds of women break through challenging life transitions.

She is the author of The Post Nest Plan, 10 Reasons You May Not Be Happy and 10 Remedies So You Can Be, 12 Steps to Self-Empowerment, creator of the Self Inventory for the Savvy Sisterhood workshop, has contributed to self-help features for Cleo and Cosmopolitan magazines in Australia, wrote the weekly Life Matters column for an Australian newspaper, and penned the viral quote *"Your perception of me is a reflection of you; my reaction to you is an awareness of me"* in June 2012.

She knows her purpose, and it is this: *"You matter in this world. If I'm going to help myself, I'll help you, too."*

Her style, content, and delivery stem from her experience of going through challenges similar to her audience, using her expertise to coach herself through them, and then bringing those self-inventory techniques and newfound awareness to struggling women.

She brings humor, self-deprecation and realness, empathy, a deep and personal understanding of pain, and the 'Australian mateship' attitude: the bonds of loyalty, equality, and feelings of solidarity and sisterhood.

She chooses to live by three words: 'onwards,' 'upwards,' and 'always.'

These words have always been 'waiting in the wings' through challenging and traumatic times and are even more significant now she finds herself as an empty nest mom in Ohio while her children have grown and flown back to her home of Australia.

Learn More:

Visit Bobbi's website at inspiredemptynest.com

Listen to the Podcast:

The Fly Mom, Fly! podcast is found at flymomfly.com and on all your favorite streaming apps.

Get In Touch:

Bobbi is available as a podcast guest, for media contributions, speaking events, and personal coaching. With her years of experience and expertise in the field of personal development, she is committed to helping women transition through the empty nest phase and rediscover their purpose and passion.

If you are interested in booking Bobbi for an event or media contribution, please email bobbi@inspiredemptynest.com